Voltaire's

PHILOSOPHICAL
DICTIONARY

Voltaire's

PHILOSOPHICAL DICTIONARY

A Compendium

Edited and Translated by

WADE BASKIN

WISDOM LIBRARY

a division of
PHILOSOPHICAL LIBRARY
New York

Library of Congress Catalog Card No. 61-17971

Printed in the United States of America

Voltaire's

PHILOSOPHICAL
DICTIONARY

FOREWORD

Abbé, the first entry in the present compendium, recalls an episode that took place almost two hundred years ago. It was in Abbeville—and probably with the approval of the local abbé—that one of Voltaire's early admirers was publicly burned in 1765, one year after the publication of the original work, for having dared to put into practice ideas advanced by his mentor. The indiscreet admirer, the young Chevalier de la Barre, had refused to uncover and kneel in the presence of a religious procession. He was found guilty of irreverence. He was then tortured and his tongue was ripped out. After he was beheaded, his body was committed to the flames. Into the bonfire his executioners threw the book that inspired his crime—Voltaire's *Philosophical Dictionary.*

That the *Philosophical Dictionary* is an important document in the history of France and a priceless contribution to the history of ideas is common knowledge, but that it refutes many distorted notions about its author merits re-emphasis. Voltaire has been variously portrayed as Catholic or atheist, deist or mystic, adulator or critic, conservative or radical, cynic or humanitarian. While there may never be a consensus with respect to his philosophy or his character, the facts and ideas set down in his *Dictionary* offer a representative sampling of his prodigious output and provide ample material for censor and defender alike. Though it is not always possible to determine at first glance whether a particular statement is to be taken at face value or to be treated with mock seriousness (here as in his other writings disclaimers are designed to protect the author rather than to enlighten the reader), the work as a whole militates against the popular conception of Voltaire as a tactless courtier and fawning libertine whose reasoning was more brilliant than sound and whose opinions changed with his moods. The facile clichés about him contrived by admirers and detractors seem crude when his statements are read in the light of the circumstances that elicited them and his views on crucial issues are reduced to their essentials. Underneath the mask of the Voltaire legend we find nothing to justify the summary treatment accorded him in a dictionary later compiled by Flaubert: "VOLTAIRE. Famous for his hideous grin or *rictus*. A superficial mind." Nor is there justification for Carlyle's complaint about "his inborn levity of nature, his entire want of Earnestness," for what is left unsaid is often as important as a belabored point. When Voltaire assures us, for example, that he merely wants to cultivate his garden, a host of evidence points to the conclusion that he claims as his garden much of the world's territory.

The earliest version of the *Dictionary* (1764) was soon followed by numerous others. Of all the other versions that appeared during Voltaire's lifetime, however, only five entailed corrections, additions, or deletions. It was the fifth of these (Geneva, 1769) that in subsequent printings was entitled *Philosophical Dictionary*. Much confusion arose when many of the articles first published in one of the six different editions of the *Dictionary* were reprinted in *Questions on the Encyclopedia*, for some were reprinted exactly as they had appeared earlier while others were revised or entirely rewritten except for the title. To further complicate matters, during the publication of his complete works (*Oeuvres complètes*, 1770-1778) articles from both the *Dictionary* and *Questions* were lumped together indiscriminately. The confusion that had arisen during his lifetime increased after his death, with the result that there is available today no authoritative English version of the *Philosophical Dictionary* as it was when Voltaire placed on it his final stamp of approval.

In these brief pages I have tried to present the essence of Voltaire's thinking on each issue dealt with in his monumental *Dictionary*. In the attempt to be systematic, I have undoubtedly failed in many instances to strike the right balance. I was tempted to reject outright dull or insignificant entries and to include only articles of compelling interest, to give more space to ideas toward which I am sympathetic and to reject those I find objectionable and to gloss over or embellish vulgarities. Perhaps displeased readers will turn to my source (the Garnier edition of the complete work) and reserve the bonfire for those who have perpetuated the Voltaire legend.

In editing and translating Voltaire's work, I have had the generous help and encouragement of all my colleagues. Dr. Donald N. Brown and Dr. Eugene E. Slaughter offered sound advice and helpful criticism on specific points. Miss Amy Aston typed and arranged the entries, checked references and helped to prepare the index. Miss Mildred Riling read through the entire manuscript and made many constructive suggestions. Dr. Margaret C. O'Riley assisted in checking the proofs. While I have benefited from their advice and criticism in editing and translating this compendium, my colleagues are in no way responsible for its shortcomings.

Southeastern State College   WADE BASKIN

A = anticlerical.

ABBÉ

The word abbé means father. If you become a father biologically, you render a service to the state; you can be sure that you are doing the best thing a man can do, for you are engendering a thinking being. There is in this act an element of the divine. But if you are Monsieur l'Abbé only because you have had your head shaved, because you wear a small collar and a short cloak, and because you expect a lucrative benefice, you do not deserve the name of abbé. The old monks gave this title to the superior whom they elected. The abbé was their spiritual father. But how the meanings of words change with time! The spiritual abbé was a poor man in charge of others equally poor. For the last two hundred years, however, the poor spiritual fathers have had incomes of two hundred or four hundred thousand pounds, and in Germany today there are poor spiritual fathers who have their own armed regiments. . . .

I hear abbés in Italy, Germany, Flanders, and Burgundy saying: "Why should we not accumulate wealth and honors? Why should we not be princes? Our bishops are. They were originally poor like us; they have enriched and elevated themselves; one of them became superior even to kings; allow us, insofar as we can, to imitate them."

Gentlemen, you are right. You should lay claim to the earth; it belongs to men with the strength and the skill to acquire it. You have used ignorance, superstition, and strife to strip us of our legacies and trample us under your feet while you waxed fat on the resources of the unfortunate. Tremble, for the day of reckoning is at hand.

ABRAHAM

Abraham is a name that was famous in Asia Minor and in Arabia, just as Thoth was famous among the Egyptians, the first Zoroaster in Persia, Hercules in Greece, Orpheus in Thrace, Odin in the northern countries, and numerous others better known by their fame than by any authentic historical account. I speak here only of profane history, for the history of the Jews, our masters and our enemies, whom we believe and whom we detest, was obviously written by the Holy Ghost; and we of course look upon it with appropriate reverence. Here we are addressing only the Arabs; they pride themselves on descending from Abraham through Ishmael; they believe that Ishmael built Mecca and died there. The fact is that the race of Ishmael has been infinitely more favored by God than the race of Jacob. Both races have, in truth, produced robbers; but the Arabian robbers have been vastly superior to the Jewish ones. Jacob's descendants conquered only a very small country which they lost; Ishmael's descendants, however, conquered parts of Asia, Europe, and Africa, established an empire more extensive than that of the Romans, and drove the Jews from their caves which they called the Promised Land. . . .

Commentators have written a prodigious number of volumes to justify Abraham's conduct and to explain away errors in chronology. We refer the reader to these commentaries; they were all composed by the incisive minds of excellent metaphysicians, men free from prejudices and pedantry.

ADAM

The pious Madame de Bourignon was sure that Adam was a hermaphrodite like the immortal Plato's first man. God had revealed to her this great secret; but since I haven't had such revelations, I shall have nothing to say on this matter. The Jewish rabbis have read Adam's books and know the name of his preceptor and of his second wife; but since I haven't read our first father's books, I shall say nothing on this matter. Some capacious and very learned minds are astonished on reading the *Veidam* of the ancient Brahmins and learning that the first man was created in India, etc., that his name was Adimo, meaning "the begetter," and that his wife was named Pocriti, meaning "life." They say that the Brahmin sect is surely more ancient than the Jewish sect; that it was not until a late period that the Jews learned to write in the Canaanite language, since it was not until the late period that they settled in the small land of Canaan. They say that the Indians were always the inventors and the Jews always the imitators; the Indians always ingenious and the Jews always uncouth. They find it hard to accept the fact that Adam, who was fair and who had no hair on his head, fathered Negroes, who are as black as ink and whose heads are covered by black wool. In fact, they leave little unsaid. But I say nothing, leaving these investigations to the Reverend Father Berruyer of the Society of Jesus. He is the most

9

ingenious man that I have ever known. His book was burned because it was thought that he was trying to ridicule the Bible, but I assure you that he had no such subtle intention.

ANGEL

"Angel" in Greek is messenger. We are hardly the wiser for being told that the Persians had their *peris,* the Hebrews, their *malakim,* and the Greeks their *daimonoi.* More cogent, perhaps, is the fact that man has always tended to place intermediate beings between himself and the divinity; such were the demons, the spirits invented in ancient times. Man has always fashioned gods in his own image. He saw princes communicating their orders through messengers and assumed that the divinity also had couriers. Mercury and Iris were couriers, or messengers. . . .

The story of the fall of the angels is not found in the books of Moses. It is first mentioned by Isaiah, who, apostrophizing the king of Babylon, exclaims, "Where is now the exactor of tributes? The pines and cedars rejoice in his fall. How hast thou fallen from heaven, oh Hellel, star of morning?" Hellel was translated by the Latin word Lucifer; afterwards in an allegorical sense, the name Lucifer was given to the prince of the warring angels in heaven; and finally this name, which means light and dawn, became the name of the devil.

The Christian religion is grounded on the fall of the angels. The angels who revolted fell from the spheres which they inhabited into hell in the center of the earth, where they became devils. A devil in the form of the serpent tempted Eve and damned mankind. Jesus came to redeem mankind and to triumph over the devil, who tempts us still. Yet this basic tradition is found only in the apocryphal book of Enoch.

And even here the version given is quite different from the accepted one. . . .

The exact dwelling place of the angels is unknown. God did not see fit to tell us whether they dwell in the air, in the void, or in the other planets.

ANTI-TRINITARIANS

Anti-Trinitarians maintain that nothing is more contrary to logic than what is taught among Christians concerning the trinity of persons in a single divine essence: that the second is begotten by the first, and the third proceeds from the other two persons; that this unintelligible doctrine is nowhere to be found in Scripture; that without departing in any way from the spirit of the text, it is possible to give to every passage on which the doctrine is based a clearer, more natural meaning and one that will conform more closely to common notions and to simple immutable truths; that to believe as their adversaries do that there are several distinct *persons* in the divine essence, and that the eternal is not the only true God but that the Son and the Holy Ghost are joined with him, is to introduce into the church of Christ the most gross and dangerous error since it is openly to advance polytheism. . . . From all this they conclude that it would be wiser to accept the authority of the apostles, who never mentioned the Trinity, and to banish forever from religion all terms which are not in Scripture, such as *trinity, person, essence, hypostasis, hypostatic* and *personal union, incarnation, generation, profession,* and a great many other terms which are absolutely devoid of meaning since in nature they are represented by no real existence; and which, therefore, evoke nothing but false, vague, obscure and uncertain notions.

APIS

Was Apis worshipped at Memphis as a god, as a symbol, or as an ox? In all probability, the fanatics looked upon him as a god, the wise as nothing more than a symbol, and the common people as only an object of worship. Was it right for Cambyses to kill this ox with his own hand? Indeed it was, for in so doing, he showed the imbeciles that their god could be put on the spit without Nature's arming herself to avenge the sacrilege. The Egyptians have been the object of much praise. I would be hard put to name a more wretched people. . . . Praise is lavished on their pyramids, but these are the monuments of an enslaved people. If the whole nation had not been set to work on them, it would have been impossible to raise those unsightly masses. And what purpose did they serve? To preserve in a small chamber the mummy of some prince or governor or official whose soul was to reanimate the mummy after a thousand years. But if they believed in the resurrection of the body, why did they remove the brain before embalming it? Were the Egyptians to be resurrected without brains?

APOCALYPSE

Justin the Martyr, who wrote about A.D. 270, was the first to speak of the Apocalypse, which he attributed to the apostle John the Evangelist. In his dialog with Tryphon, he was asked by the Jew if he did not believe that Jerusalem was one day to be re-established. Justin replied that he, like all other devout Christians, thought that it was to be. "There was among us," he said, "a certain person named John, one of the twelve apostles of Jesus. According to his prediction, the faithful will spend a thousand years in Jerusalem. . . ."

The same St. Justin confidently cited the sibyllic oracles. Going even further, he pretended to have seen the remains of the little dwellings in which the seventy-two interpreters were confined in the Egyptian pharos in the time of Herod. The fact that he had the misfortune to see these places suggests that he might possibly have been confined there himself. . . .

Every Christian community has applied to itself the prophecies contained in this book. In it the English have found the revolutions of Great Britain; the Lutherans, the troubles of Germany; the French Protestants, the reign of Charles IX and the regency of Catherine de Medici. All of them are equally right. Bossuet and Newton both commented on the Apocalypse. The truth is, however, that the eloquent declamations of the first and the sublime discoveries of the second have brought them greater renown than their commentaries on the Apocalypse.

ARIUS

The incomprehensible doctrine of Arianism for more than sixteen hundred years has given free reign to sophistic subtlety, to bitterness, to intrigue, to the urge to dominate and to persecute, to blind and sanguinary fanaticism, to barbarous credulity. It has produced more horrors than the ambition of princes, which has produced a goodly number. Is Jesus the Word? If he is the Word, did he emanate from God in time or before time? If he emanated from God, is he co-eternal and co-substantial with Him, or is he of a similar substance? Is he or is he not distinguished from God? Is he made or begotten . . . and how is it that if he has exactly the same nature, the same essence as the Father and the Son, he cannot do the same things as these two persons who are himself? This I cannot understand; no one has ever understood it, and that is why so many people have been butchered.

The Christians practiced sophistry, quibbled among themselves, despised and excommunicated one another before the time of Arius and Athanasius on account of some of these incomprehensible dogmas. The Egyptian Greeks were clever enough to split a hair into four, but in the matter of the godhead they split it only into three. Alexandros, bishop of Alexandria, saw fit to preach that God was necessarily individual and indivisible, that he was a monad in the strictest sense of the word, and that this monad was triune. Alexandros' monad scandalized the priest Arius, who offered a different explanation. . . . Alexandros quickly assembled a small council of those who shared his opinion and excommunicated his priest. . . . The emperor Constantine was a villain. . . . He sent the celebrated bishop Osius with conciliatory letters to the two warring factions. . . . But Osius was confronted by an obstinate audience. The Council of Nicaea was assembled and war raged throughout the Roman Empire. This civil war led to others, and from century to century to this day, internecine persecution has continued.

ATHEISM

Once anyone who possessed a secret in any of the arts ran the risk of being looked upon as a sorcerer. Every new sect was charged with murdering infants in its mysterious rites, and every philosopher who deviated from the accepted jargon was accused of atheism by fanatics and knaves and condemned by fools. . . .

The laws of Moses did not teach the doctrine of a future life, did not threaten with punishment after death, did not even teach the primitive Jews the immortality of the soul; but the Jews, far from being atheists, far from believing that they could eschew divine vengeance, were the most religious of men. . . .

But among the Gentiles, various sects knew no restraint. The skeptics had doubts about everything, and the academicians suspended judgment. The Epicureans were persuaded that the divinity could not meddle in the affairs of men, and in their hearts there was room for no divinity. . . .

Atheists are for the most part venturesome but misguided men of learning who reason badly, and who, unable to understand creation, the origin of evil and other abstruse issues, have recourse to the hypothesis of the eternity of things and necessity. . . . We should add that there are fewer atheists today than ever before, for philosophers now realize that there is no vegetative being without a germ, no germ without a pattern, etc., and that grain does not spring from decayed matter. Unphilosophical geometrists have rejected final causes, but true philosophers accept them; and as a well-known author has observed, "A catechist announced God to children and Newton demonstrates Him to the wise."

B

BABEL

Vanity has always raised great monuments. It was because of vanity that men built the lofty tower of Babel. "Let us go and raise a tower, the summit of which shall touch the skies and render our name celebrated before we are scattered upon the face of the earth." The enterprise was begun in the time of a patriarch named Phaleg, who had for his fifth ancestor the good man Noah. Architecture and all its accompanying arts had obviously made great progress in five generations. St. Jerome, the same man who saw fauns and satyrs, did not see the tower of Babylon any more than I have seen it; and yet he assures us that it was twenty thousand feet high.

BAPTISM

Baptism is a Greek word that means immersion. Men, always guided by their senses, imagined that what purified the body also purified the soul. Beneath the Egyptian temple were huge tubs for the priests and the initiated. From time immemorial the Indians have plunged into the Ganges, and this ceremony is still in vogue. The Hebrews adopted the ceremony of baptism for all foreigners embraced by the Judaic law who were unwilling to submit to circumcision. . . .

John baptized in the Jordan. He even baptized Jesus, who never baptized anyone, but who, nevertheless, deigned to consecrate this ancient ceremony. Every sign is neutral in itself and God attaches his grace to the sign of his choice. Baptism soon became the chief rite and the seal of the Christian religion. Still, though the first fifteen bishops were all circumcised, it has not been established that they were baptized.

The sacrament was abused during the early centuries of Christianity; nothing was more common than to postpone the receiving of baptism until the last agony. The Emperor Constantine's example is a very good proof of this. Here is how he reasoned: "Baptism purifies everything; I can therefore kill my wife, my son, and all my relatives; after that I can be baptized and I shall go to heaven." And he acted accordingly. Gradually people abolished the custom of waiting until death to step into the sacred bath. . . .

In the second century infant baptism began. It was natural for Christians to want their children, who would otherwise have been damned, to have this sacrament. Finally it was decided that it should be administered at the end of eight days, because among the Jews this was the age for circumcision. . . .

The Quakers, who comprise a numerous society in England and America, do not use baptism because Jesus Christ did not baptize any of his disciples, and they aim to be Christians only as his disciples were, which sets them apart from all other communions.

BEASTS

Beasts have wrongly been treated as mechanical creatures with neither intelligence nor sensation. They are said to follow a fixed pattern of behavior, to be incapable of learning or acquiring skills. But is a bird following a fixed pattern of behavior when it varies the shape of its nest—a semicircle for a wall, a quarter circle for a corner, or a full circle for a tree? If you try for three months to train a hound to hunt, doesn't he learn something? Does a canary repeat a tune at first hearing or only after a long period of instruction?

BEAUTY

Ask a toad what beauty is—the great beauty, *To Kalon.* He will answer that beauty is his mate with her two big round eyes bulging out of her little head, her wide flat mouth, her yellow belly, and her brown back. Ask a Negro from Guinea. Beauty is to him a black, oily skin, sunken eyes, and a flat nose. Ask the devil. He will tell you that a pair of horns, four claws, and a tail constitute beauty. Finally, consult the philosophers and they will give you a silly answer; they must have something that corresponds to the archetype of essential beauty—to the *To Kalon.*

Once I was with a philosopher during the performance of a tragedy. "How beautiful it is!" he said. "What do you find beautiful in it?" I asked. "The fact that the author fulfilled his purpose." The next day he took some medicine which did him some good. "It has fulfilled its purpose," I told him. "It is really a beautiful medicine." Then he understood that medicine cannot be called beautiful and that the word beauty can be applied to a thing only if it evokes admiration and pleasure. He agreed that the tragedy had inspired in him both sentiments, and that it was, therefore, the *To Kalon*, the beautiful.

We took a trip to England, where the same tragedy was being presented. Though the translation was perfect, all the spectators were yawning. "Oh, oh," he said, "the *To Kalon* is not the same for the English as for the French." He concluded, after much reflection, that beauty is often relative; that what is decent in Japan is indecent in Rome; that what is fashionable in Paris is not so in Peking. He was spared the ordeal of composing a long treatise on beauty.

BLIND SPOTS

Few men will consistently mistake a rooster for a horse or a chamber pot for a house. Why do some men who think clearly on other matters have a blind spot with respect to certain important issues? Why does the Siamese, who is never deceived in a matter involving the payment of three rupees, persist in believing in the metamorphoses of Sammonocodom? Through what strange quirk do sensible men behave like Don Quixote, who believed that he saw giants where other men could see only windmills. . . ?

The greatest geniuses can have a blind spot with respect to a principle which they have accepted without question. Newton showed extremely bad judgment in his commentary on the Apocalypse.

BODY

All of us resemble the average Parisian lady who eats well but who never knows exactly what goes into the stew. We all have bodies, but we do not know their composition. Of what does a body consist? Of parts, and these parts are composed of other parts. And what are these other parts? They, too, are bodies. We may continue to divide substance without making the slightest progress. A subtle philosopher noticed that a picture was made of ingredients, but that none of the ingredients was a picture; that a house was made of materials but that none of the materials was a house. He concluded that bodies were composed of an infinite number of small beings which were not bodies, and these he called monads. His system is not without merit. . . . It is as good as the next one. I like it as well as the declension of atoms, or substantial forms, or versatile grace, or Don Calmet's vampires.

C

CANNIBALS

We find evidence of cannibalism in America and elsewhere in the modern world. Nor were the Cyclops the only individuals in antiquity to feed on human flesh. Juvenal relates that among the Egyptians, a wise people renowned for their laws—and pious worshipers of crocodiles and onions—the Tentyrites ate an enemy who had fallen into their hands. His report is not founded on hearsay, for the crime was committed almost before his eyes. . . . Though we no longer practice cannibalism, we kill our neighbors on the battlefield and in skirmishes, and for the most trivial reason we provide meals for crows and worms. There is the horror; there is the crime. Yet what does it matter when a man is dead whether he is eaten by a soldier or whether he is eaten by a crow or a dog?

In general we show more respect for the dead than for the living. Both merit our respect. The so-called civilized nations have done right in not putting their vanquished on the spit. If we were allowed to eat our neighbors, we would soon be eating our fellow citizens—and this would be unpatriotic.

CATECHISM OF THE CHINESE

CU-SU. I shall not repeat to you every trite statement which we have made over the past five or six thousand years on every single virtue. Some of them, like prudence, for the guidance of our souls, and temperance for our physical well-being, are our exclusive property; they are precepts relating to politics and health. True virtues are those useful to society, such as faithfulness, magnanimity, kindliness, and tolerance. Thank heaven not a single old woman among us fails to teach these virtues to her grandchildren; they come first in the education of our young people in villages as well as in cities. . . .

How wise and saintly was our Confucius! Not one single virtue does he fail to inspire. The happiness of mankind is at the crux of each of his maxims. Here is one that comes to mind. It is the fifty-third: "One good deed deserves another, but no wrong should ever be repaid in kind. . . ."

KOU. I have read everything written by Confucius and the sages of past centuries on humility, but it seems to me that they have never precisely defined it. . . .

CU-SU. Humility is not abjection. It tempers self-love as modesty tempers pride.

KOU. In my own life, I would like to practice all these virtues and worship one universal God far from the chimeras of the sophists and the illusions of the false prophets. Love of my neighbor would be my cardinal virtue and love of God my religion. . . . The divinity speaks to the hearts of all men, and bonds of charity ought to unite them all from one end of the universe to the other.

CATECHISM OF THE CURATE

ARISTON. You are a scholar and an eloquent speaker. How do you expect to preach to country people?

THÉOTIME. As I would preach to kings. I shall always speak of morals and never of controversy. . . . I shall try to mold good men and to be a good man; but I shall not turn out theologians, and I shall be as little theological as possible.

ARISTON. Oh, you are a good curate. I want to buy a cottage in your parish. Please tell me how you will handle confessions.

THÉOTIME. Confession is an excellent thing, invented in the most remote times to check crimes. Confession played a part in the celebration of all the ancient mysteries. We have imitated and sanctified this sage practice. It is a very good device for wringing forgiveness from hearts ulcerated by hate, and for making petty thieves return what they may have stolen from their neighbors. It has some drawbacks. There are many indiscreet confessors, especially among monks, who sometimes teach girls more foolishness than all the village boys could possibly teach them. . . .

ARISTON. And would you make use of excommunications?

THÉOTIME. No, there are rituals for excommunicating grasshoppers, sorcerers, and comedians. I would not prohibit grasshoppers from entering the church, since they never go there anyway; nor would I excommunicate sorcerers, since there are none; and with respect to comedians, since they are pensioned by the king and authorized by the magistrates, I would avoid defaming them. . . .

ARISTON. The more you reveal to me your sentiments, the more I wish to become your parishioner. But there is still one important point that bothers me. What would you do to keep the peasants from becoming intoxicated every feast day. . . ?

THÉOTIME. I have thought of that. I would allow feasts, and I would even encourage them to work in their fields on feast days after the divine service, which I would conduct early in the day. The thing that brings them to the tavern on holidays is idleness. Workdays are not days of debauchery and murder. Work in moderation contributes to physical and spiritual well-being; moreover, work is necessary for the state. . . .

ARISTON. So you would reconcile praying and working: God prescribes both. You would serve both God and your neighbor. But in ecclesiastical disputes, which side would you take?

THÉOTIME. None. There can be no dispute concerning virtue, because it originates in God. People quarrel about opinions, which originate in men.

CATECHISM OF THE GARDENER

TUCTAN. I would like to learn what your principles are.

KARPOS. To be, for example, a good husband, a good father, a good neighbor, a good subject, and a good gardener. I go no further than that, and I hope that God will show me mercy.

TUCTAN. And do you think that he will show mercy to me, the governor of your island?

KARPOS. How do you expect me to know that? Am I to divine how God disposes of governors? That is between you and him; I have nothing to do with it. All that I can say is that if you are as good a governor as I am a gardener, then I suppose God will treat you well.

TUCTAN. By Mohammed, I like that idolater. Good-bye, my friend. May Allah keep you under his holy protection.

KARPOS. Thank you very much. May Theos have pity on you, dear governor.

CATECHISM OF THE JAPANESE

THE JAPANESE. The Quakers merit particular attention. They are the only guests whom I have never seen drinking and swearing. They are hard to deceive; but they never practice deceit. It seems that the law "Thou shalt love thy neighbor as thyself" was made just for these people. . . . They say that poor mortals are but clay pitchers made to last but a short time, and that there is no reason for them to go about deliberately destroying each other. I confess that, if I were not a Canusi, I would not mind being a Quaker. . . .

THE INDIAN. People have too many prejudices—national, political, and personal.

THE JAPANESE. You are right. They have too many prejudices.

CERTAIN—CERTAINTY

A young man beginning the study of geometry came to me; he had not yet reached the definition of triangles. "Aren't you certain," I asked, "that the three angles of a triangle are equal to two right angles?" He answered that he was not certain and that furthermore, he had not even the slightest notion of the proposition. I demonstrated it to him. He then became very certain of it, and he will remain so throughout his life. . . . Mathematical certainty is immutable and eternal.

I exist, I think, I feel pain—is all that just as certain as a geometrical truth? Why? Because these truths are proved by the principle that it is impossible for a thing to exist and at the same time not to exist. I cannot simultaneously exist and not exist, or feel and not feel. A triangle cannot at the same time contain one hundred and eighty degrees, the sum of two right angles, and not contain them. The physical certainty of my existence and my feeling is like mathematical certainty, but of a different type. The same does not hold true for certainty grounded on appearance or on the unanimous testimony of mankind.

CHAIN OF BEING

On first reading Plato and seeing the gradation of being extending from the lightest atom to the Supreme Being, I was filled with admiration. Like the apparitions of old that vanished with the crowing of the cock, however, this great phantom could not bear the light of careful examination. The imagination is at first pleased with the imperceptible transition from brute matter to organized substance, from plants to zoophytes, from zoophytes to animals, from animals to men, from men to genii, from genii with light, ethereal bodies to immaterial substances, and finally to a thousand orders of these substances which spanning the gap between beauty and perfection, ascend to God Himself. . . . But there is a greater distance between God and his most perfect creatures than between the Holy Father and the dean of the Sacred College. The dean may become a pope, but the most perfect genii created by the Supreme Being cannot become God. Between him and God lies infinity.

CHAIN OF EVENTS

It has long been held that all events are chained together by an invincible fatality. This is Destiny, which in Homer is superior to Jupiter himself. . . . The doctrine of necessity and fatality which Leibniz claims to have invented in our own times—his so-called pre-established harmony—is actually very old. That there is no effect without a cause and that often the smallest cause produces the greatest effects, is not restricted to our times. . . .

The movement of the smallest atom has influenced the present structure of the whole world; and the most insignificant accident, whether among men or among animals, is an essential link in the great chain of destiny. The facts are clear. Every effect has an obvious cause, and this cause can be traced backward to the abyss of eternity; but not every cause has an effect that reaches to the end of time. I agree that all events are produced by other events. The past has given birth to the present and the present will give birth to the future. Every man has a father, but not every man is a father. . . . Present events are not the offspring of all past events. They are tied directly to certain events, but with a thousand small collateral chains they have nothing in common. Once more it should be noted that every being has a parent but that not every being has an offspring.

CHARACTER

Character is from the Greek word meaning impression or engraving. It is what nature has engraved in us. The question is, can we change our character? If I have a hooked nose and cat eyes, I can hide them with a mask. Can I do the same in the case of the character given me by nature? A man violent and impulsive by nature came before Francis I, King of France, to complain about a trespass. The king's countenance, the respectful behavior of his courtiers, and the surroundings made a strong impression on the man. Mechanically he cast down his eyes, softened his rude voice, and humbly presented his petition. At that particular moment he seemed as mild as the courtiers who were the cause of his submissiveness. But Francis I, well versed in physiognomy, saw the somber fire that lit his downcast eyes, the tense muscles in his face, and the rigidity of his sealed lips. He realized that this man was not so mild as he was forced to appear. The same man followed him to Pavia, was taken prisoner with him, and was taken with him to Madrid. No longer was he awed by the majesty of Francis I, for he had become familiar with the object of his reverence. One day, while pulling on the king's boots, he happened to make a wrong pull; and the king, embittered by misfortune, grew angry. The man threw the boots out the window and would have nothing more to do with the king. . . .

Religion and morality curb nature; they do not destroy it. . . . Age weakens character. . . . To try to animate a lazy man and urge him on to persevering activity, to calm and soothe an impetuous man, to inspire a taste for poetry in a man who has neither the taste nor the ear for it would be as futile as to attempt to give sight to a man who was born blind. We can perfect, we can better, we can hide what nature has instilled in us; but we can instill nothing in ourselves.

CHINA

We should not overemphasize the merits of the Chinese. The constitution of their empire is the only one based entirely upon paternal authority; the only one which provides punishment for a provincial governor who fails at the end of his tenure to receive the acclamations of the people; the only one which rewards virtue (in all others the sole object of legislation is the punishment of crime); the only one which has caused its conquerors to adopt its laws. . . . But with respect to the sciences the Chinese lag two hundred years behind us. Furthermore, they labor, like us, under a thousand ridiculous prejudices and, as we long did ourselves, they believe in magic and in judicial astrology. . . . Even so, four thousand years ago, before we had learned to read, the Chinese knew everything essentially useful which we pride ourselves on knowing today.

The religion of the literate people—this bears repetition—commands admiration. It is free from superstitions, absurd legends, and dogmas that are an insult to reason and to nature. . . . Throughout more than forty centuries the simplest form of worship has appeared to them the best. They are much as we conceive Seth, Enoch, and Noah to have been. Along with all the sages of the world, they are contented to adore one god; in contrast to this, Europe is torn between Thomas and Bonaventure, between Calvin and Luther, between Jansenius and Molina.

CHRISTIANITY

Jesus was born under the Mosaic Law. He was circumcised according to the law; He fulfilled all the precepts of the law and kept all its feasts. He preached only ethics. He never revealed the mystery of His incarnation or told the Jews that He was born of a virgin. In the waters of the Jordan He received John's benediction. Though a number of Jews submitted to the baptismal ceremony, He never baptized anyone. He did not speak of the seven sacraments, nor did He institute an ecclesiastical hierarchy of any type during His life. He concealed from His contemporaries that He was the Son of God, begotten from the foundation of the world, consubstantial with God, and that the Holy Ghost proceeded from the Father and the Son. He did not say that His person was composed of two natures and of two wills. He saw fit to have these mysteries announced to men in the course of time by those who were to be illuminated by the Holy Ghost. Never during His life did He deviate from the law of His fathers. To all others He was simply a just man, pleasing to God, persecuted by those who envied Him, and condemned to death by prejudiced magistrates. . . .

The name Christian was given to the faithful in Antioch around the year 60 of our vulgar era, but they were known in the Roman Empire by other names. . . . God, who descended to the earth in order to serve as an example of humility and poverty, thus gave to His church the most humble beginnings and charted its course in accordance with the humble state into which He had seen fit to be born. . . .

It was around the year A.D. 60 that the Christians began to set themselves apart from the Jewish communion, and this separation was the cause of many quarrels and persecutions. Their Jewish brethren, who had established synagogues in

Rome, in Greece, in Egypt, and in Asia—accused them of impiety and atheism, and excommunicated them three times every Sabbath day. But God always upheld them in the midst of their persecutions. Several Christian churches gradually evolved, and complete separation of the Jews and the Christians was accomplished before the end of the first century. . . .

When the Christian societies became more numerous and several of them rebelled against worshipping the Roman Empire, the magistrates acted cruelly toward them, and other people were quick to persecute them. The Jews, who had special privileges and who locked themselves in their synagogues, were not persecuted. They were allowed to practice their religion just as they still are today in Rome. All other religions in the far-flung empire were tolerated, though the Senate did not adopt them. But the Christians, avowed enemies of every other form of worship and especially of worshipping the empire, were frequently exposed to cruel torture. . . . Through the ages there were so many martyrs that care must be exercised in separating the true history of those who died for their religion from the dangerous hodgepodge of fables and false martyrs. . . .

The whole of Asia and Africa, half of Europe, all the possessions of the English and the Dutch, the vast numbers of unconquered Americans, and all the austral lands which make up one-fifth of the globe are still prey to the devil. This bears out the Scripture, "Many are called but few are chosen." Some of our learned men say that there are on the earth approximately sixteen hundred million men; if this is true, the universal Holy Roman Catholic Church has about sixty million of them—more than $1/26$ of the inhabitants of the known world.

CIRCUMCISION

Many nations adopted circumcision from Egypt, but none has ever pretended to have received it from the Jews. To whom then can we attribute the origin of this custom? Did it originate in a nation from whom five or six others acknowledge that they took it? Or did it originate in another nation much less powerful, less commercial, and less warlike, a nation hidden away in a corner of Arabia Petraea, which has never communicated to any other nation a single one of its customs? The Jews say that the Egyptians once condescended to give them a home. In all probability, the minority race imitated the custom of the majority race, with the result that the Jews adopted certain practices from their masters. . . .

That God, who sanctified baptism, an ancient practice among Asians, should also have sanctified circumcision, an equally ancient practice among Africans, is in no way extraordinary. It has already been noted that He has a sovereign right to attach His grace to the symbol of His choice.

COMMON SENSE

It is sometimes said that common sense is very rare. What is the meaning of this statement? That in many men certain prejudices check the development of incipient reason; that a man who exercises sound judgment in one instance will always blunder in another.

An Arab may be a good mathematician, a learned chemist, and an accomplished astronomer, and still believe that Mohammed has half of the moon in his sleeve. Why does he excel in the three sciences mentioned and go so far astray on the issue of the half moon? The reason is that in the first instance, he has seen through his own eyes and perfected his intelligence; in the second, he has closed his eyes, seen through the eyes of others, and perverted his innate common sense.

CONFESSION

Confession was practiced in all the mysteries of Isis, Orpheus, and Ceres. People confessed to the hierophant and to the initiated. These mysteries were expiations; and people did, of course, have crimes to expiate.

The Christians adopted the confession during the first centuries of the church, just as they took over almost all the rites of antiquity, along with temples, altars, incense, candles, processions, lustral water, priestly robes, and various formulas of the mysteries—the *Sursum corda,* the *Ite missa est,* and a number of others. The scandal of the public confession of a woman, when it reached Constantinople in the fourth century, caused the abolition of the confession.

The practice of having one man confess in secret to another man was not adopted in the West until around the seventh century, when abbots began to require their monks to come before them twice each year and acknowledge their shortcomings. These abbots invented the formula, "in thy need I absolve thee to the utmost of my power." It seems that it would have been more respectful towards the Supreme Being and more appropriate to say, "May He forgive your shortcomings and mine!"

CONVULSIONS

The Jansenists, to prove beyond doubt that Jesus Christ could never have assumed the habit of a Jesuit, treated Paris to an orgy of miraculous convulsions and drew great numbers of spectators. Carré de Montgeron, a parliamentary counselor, went to present to the king a quarto collection of these astounding events, which had been verified by a thousand witnesses. He was summarily imprisoned in a castle, where an attempt was made to restore his sanity; but truth always triumphs over persecution, and the miraculous convulsions continued without interruption during the next thirty years. . . .

A famous theologian even had the benefit of being crucified for the purpose of convincing the world that a certain bill was ridiculous—something that could easily have been proven without so much trouble. But both the Jesuits and the Jansenists presented a solid front against the *Spirit of Laws* and against—and against—and against—and—. And we, after all that, dare to ridicule Laplanders, Samoyeds, and Negroes!

COUNCILS

All councils are doubtlessly infallible, for they are composed of human beings. It is impossible for passions, intrigues, cynicism, hatred, jealousy, prejudice, and ignorance to reign in these assemblies. But, why, it might be asked, have so many councils contradicted each other? To test our faith; each was right in its own time. Today Roman Catholics believe only in the councils approved in the Vatican, and Greek Orthodox Catholics believe only in those approved in Constantinople. Protestants ridicule both; everyone ought therefore to be happy. Here we shall speak only of the great councils; the little ones are not worth the bother. The first was the Council of Nicaea. The question considered was whether or not Jesus Christ was created. . . . After much discussion it was finally decided that the Son was as old as the Father and *consubstantial* with the Father. This decision is hardly intelligible, but it is for that reason all the more sublime. . . .

In 431 a great council was convoked at Ephesus. Nestorius, the bishop of Constantinople, who was a great persecutor of heretics, was himself condemned as a heretic for having maintained that Jesus Christ was indeed God, but that His mother was not the mother of God but simply the mother of Jesus Christ. . . . Here the reader should carefully note that the Gospel is silent with respect to both the consubstantiality of the Word and the honor that belonged to Mary in her role as mother of God, and that the same holds true for other disputes which have occasioned the convocation of infallible councils.

COUNTRY

A country comprises many families. . . . The more a country increases in size, the less we love it; for love is weakened by partition. It is impossible to love tenderly a family whose members are too numerous to be known intimately.

A man who is burning with ambition to be edile, tribune, praetor, consul, or dictator extolls his love for his country, yet loves only himself. Everyone wants to be sure that he can sleep in his own bed and that no other man can take it upon himself to force him to sleep elsewhere. Every man wants to be certain of his property and his life, and since all people have the same desires, the particular interest becomes the general interest. People talk about what is best for the republic, but they have at heart what is best for themselves.

Never on this earth was there a state which was not governed at the outset as a republic, for such is the natural course of human nature. . . . But which is better, to have a monarchy or a republic? The question has been debated for four thousand years. Ask the rich and they will all tell you that they prefer an aristocracy; ask the commoners and they will choose democracy; only kings prefer monarchy. How, then, is it possible for almost all the earth to be governed by monarchs? Ask the rats who proposed to hang a bell around the cat's neck. In truth, the real reason is that men are rarely worthy of governing themselves. To be a good patriot, one must unfortunately become the enemy of the rest of mankind. Old Cato, that good citizen, always proclaimed in speaking to the Senate, "I say that Carthage must be destroyed." To be a good patriot is to want our own town to become rich through commerce and to become strong through wars.

CREDO

Here I shall report the *Credo* of the abbot of Saint-Pierre as he set it down in his book on the purity of religion. His book was never printed, and I have copied it faithfully.

"I believe in but one God, whom I love. I believe that He illuminates every soul that comes into the world, just as St. John says. By that I mean every soul that seeks him in good faith. I believe in but one God because there can be but one great universal soul, but one life-giving being, but one unique Creator. I believe in God the omnipotent Father because He is the common father to all nature and to all men, who are in turn his children. . . . I believe that since God is the father of us all, we are all bound to look upon all men as our brothers. The persecutor is abominable, and he ranks next to the corruptor and the parricide. I believe that theological disputes are both farcical and ridiculous, and that they constitute the most frightful scourge on the earth, ranking next to war, pestilence, famine, and syphilis. I believe that ecclesiastics ought to be well paid—as public servants, as instructors in ethics, and as keepers of vital statistics—but that they ought to be given neither the wealth of feudal lords nor the rank of princes, because both corrupt the soul, and nothing is more revolting than to see men who are rich and proud force people who earn only a hundred crowns to preach humility and love of poverty."

CRITICISM

I do not pretend here to speak of scholiastic criticism, which restores imperfectly in an ancient text a word that was previously clearly understood; nor do I have in mind the true critics, who have untangled, insofar as possible, ancient history and ancient philosophy. I have in mind the critics who show a predilection for satire. . . . Racine's inimitable tragedies were all criticized, and very badly: they were criticized by his rivals. It is true that artists are competent judges of art, but these competent judges are almost always corrupt judges.

An excellent critic would be an artist with ample knowledge and good taste, who was free from prejudices and envy. This combination is difficult to find.

D

DAVID

I have deep respect for the worthy Jew, whoever he was, who was inspired by the God of the universe to write for the edification of the world the true history of the mighty Hebrew empire. But I am bothered by the fact that my friend David began by recruiting a band of thieves . . . and that the Lord's own anointed kidnaped Nabal, who immediately thereafter was found dead, and lost no time in marrying his widow. . . . Don Calmet justifies and sanctifies all these acts, which would cause us to shiver with horror if they were not incredible. . . .

I shall not speak here of Uriah's murder nor of Bathsheba's flagrant adultery. The ways of God are so different from the ways of men that He allowed Jesus Christ to descend from this infamous woman, everything having been in some sacred and mysterious manner made pure.

I do not question Jurieu's audacity in persecuting Bayle for not approving all the actions of the good king David. I only ask why a man like Jurieu was allowed to molest a wise man like Bayle.

DESTINY

The most ancient of all the books that have come down to us, are Homer's. In them we find the manners of profane antiquity, hardy heroes, and rude gods made in man's image. But we also find the seeds of philosophy, especially the idea of destiny, which is the master of the gods just as they are the masters of the world. . . .

Philosophers would never have required either Homer or the Pharisees to determine to their own satisfaction that everything obeys immutable laws, that everything is ordained, and that everything is, in fact, necessary. Either the world subsists by virtue of its own nature—by its own physical laws—or a supreme being shaped it according to his supreme laws. In either instance, these laws are immutable; in either instance, everything is necessary. Heavy bodies tend toward the center of the earth and cannot tend to remain in the air. Pear trees can never bear pineapples. A spaniel's instinct cannot be that of an ostrich. Everything is ordained, regulated, and circumscribed.

Man can have only a certain number of teeth, hairs, and ideas. There comes a time when a man necessarily loses his teeth, his hair, and his ideas. . . .

It would indeed be strange if one part of the world changed and the other did not; if one part of what happens had to happen and another part did not. On close examination we see that a doctrine opposed to belief in destiny is absurd, yet many people are destined to be mad thinkers, others not to think at all, and others to persecute those who think. . . .

I have necessarily the desire to write this; and you have the desire to censure me. We are both fools, both the playthings of destiny. Your nature is to do evil but mine is to love truth and to publish it in spite of you.

DIVINITY OF JESUS

The Socinians, who are regarded as blasphemers, do not recognize the divinity of Jesus Christ. They dare to pretend, along with the philosophers of antiquity, the Jews, the Mohammedans, and many other nations, that the notion of a man-god is monstrous, that the distance between God and man is infinite, and that it is impossible for the infinite, immense, and eternal Being to have been contained in a perishable body. . . .

They cite St. Paul, who never calls Jesus Christ God and who often calls Him man. They go so far as to state that the Christians devoted three whole centuries to the gradual fashioning of the apotheosis of Jesus, and that in erecting our astonishing edifice, they were merely following the example of the pagans who had deified mortals. . . . Faustus Socinus took the lead in spreading the seeds of this doctrine in Europe, and by the end of the sixteenth century the establishment of a new species of Christianity had almost been completed.

DOGMAS

All my friends will bear witness to the fact that I was transported to heaven on February 18, 1763. . . . You can well imagine my astonishment, but it may be hard for you to believe that I witnessed the judgment of the dead. And who were the judges? You will be pleased to know that they were all those who have done good to man—Confucius, Solon, Socrates, Titus, Marcus Aurelius, Antoninus Pius, and Epictetus—all the great men who, having taught and practiced the virtues which God requires, seemed to have the exclusive right to pronounce his decrees. I saw a prodigious multitude of spirits. Each of them was saying, "I believe, I believe," but on the forehead of each one was written, "I acted," and all were condemned. . . . After they had disposed of every case, I heard this proclamation: "By order of the eternal creator, preserver, rewarder, avenger, forgiver, etc., be it known to every inhabitant in the hundred thousand million billion worlds that he saw fit to create that we shall never judge any of the inhabitants by their shallow ideas, but solely by their actions. Such is our justice."

I admit this was the first time that I had ever heard such an edict. Every one of those that I had read on the little grain of sand where I was born ended with these words: "For such is our pleasure."

DREAMS

We may try in vain to prove to ourselves that memory stimulates the brain and that the brain stimulates the mind, but regardless of the system that we adopt, we must admit that all our ideals are independent of our will during sleep. . . . Dreams have always been a great object of superstition; nothing is more natural. A man deeply affected by the illness of his mistress dreams of her death; the next day she dies. He of course believes that the gods have predicted her death. . . . We remember only the dreams that are fulfilled; we forget the others.

E

ENTHUSIASM

Enthusiasm is exactly like wine. It may cause such agitation in the blood vessels and such strong vibrations in the nerves that it completely destroys reason, or it may provide only a slight stimulus which merely renders the brain more active. This activity results in great bursts of eloquence and especially in sublime poetry. Enthusiasm tempered by reason is the attribute of great poets.

Such controlled enthusiasm accounts for their perfection as artists. It is responsible for the time-honored belief that poets are inspired by the gods, a notion never applied to other artists.

How can reason control enthusiasm? A poet first outlines his composition. Reason then guides his pen. But when he wishes to breathe life into his characters and to depict their emotions; then his imagination kindles and his enthusiasm is unleashed. Like a spirited courser, it carries him forward, but in his course he follows a predetermined plan.

EQUALITY

What does one dog owe to another dog, or one horse to another horse? Nothing. No animal depends on another of its kind; but man, having received the divine spark called reason, is almost everywhere enslaved. . . . On our wretched globe it is impossible to prevent men living in society from being divided into two classes, one consisting of the rich, who command, and the other of the poor, who serve; and the two main classes are subdivided into a thousand, each with its myriad variations. . . . Every man comes into the world with a penchant for domination, riches, and pleasures, and with a strong predilection for intolerance. The result is that every man wants to possess the wealth and women or daughters of other men, to be their master, to subject them to his every whim, and to do nothing—or at least to do only what he finds perfectly agreeable. It is obviously impossible for men with such amiable dispositions to be equal, just as it is impossible for two preachers or theologians not to be jealous of each other.

EZEKIEL

Everyone knows today that ancient practices must not be judged according to modern standards. Any attempt to reform the court of Alcinous in the Odyssey and to pattern it after the court of the Grand Turk or of Louis XIV would be rejected by educated men; and anyone who found fault with Virgil for having depicted King Evander as receiving ambassadors while clad in a bear's skin and accompanied by two dogs would be a contemptible critic.

The manners of the ancient Egyptians and Jews are still more unlike ours than those of King Alcinous, his daughter, Nausicaa, and good King Evander. Ezekiel, a slave among the Chaldeans, had a vision. . . . Several critics have found unpalatable the order given by the Lord to eat for a period of 390 days bread made of barley, wheat, and millet, and spread with human excrement.

The prophet cried out, "Faugh, faugh, faugh! Until now my soul was not polluted." And the Lord answered, "Well, you may have cow dung instead of human excrement, and you may knead your bread with the dung."

Since it is not a common practice to put such confections on bread, most people find these commandments unworthy of the Divine Majesty. But we must admit that cow dung and all the great Mogul's diamonds are perfectly equal, not only in the eyes of the Divine Being, but in those of a true philosopher; and we have no right to inquire into God's reasons for prescribing such a diet for the prophet. We need simply to observe that these commandments, though they seem strange to us, did not appear so to the Jews. . . .

Any man who pronounced in the presence of others the word corresponding to *futuo* would be looked upon as a drunken lout; this word and several others used by Horace and other writers seem to us even more indecent than the expressions in Ezekiel. We must rid ourselves of all our prejudices in reading ancient writers or in traveling in distant nations. Nature is everywhere the same, but practices are everywhere different.

F

FABLES

The most ancient fables are patently allegorical. . . . The ancient fable of Venus as related by Hesiod is an allegory of nature in its entirety. The different parts of creation fell from the Ether to the edge of the sea. Venus was born from this precious scum. Her first name means lover of creation. Could any image be more meaningful? This Venus is the goddess of beauty. Beauty unaccompanied by the graces ceases to be lovely. Beauty gives birth to love. Love has arrows to pierce hearts. Love is blind to the faults of the beloved. . . .

What is true of the ancient fables is also true of our modern stories: some are instructive and charming, others are insipid.

FAITH

What is faith? Is it belief in what is evident? No, for it is evident to me that there is a necessary eternal, supreme, and intelligent Being. This is a matter not of faith but of reason. . . . Faith consists in believing not what seems true, but what seems false to our understanding. Only through faith can Asians believe in Mohammed's journey to the seven planets or in the incarnations of Vishnu, Xaca, Brahma, Sammono-codom, and the god Fo. They sacrifice understanding. They cringe before analysis. Wishing to avoid being either impaled or burned, they say, "I believe."

We have no intention here of making the slightest allusion to the Catholic faith. This we not only revere, but also possess. We refer only to the false, lying faith of other nations of the world, to the faith which is not faith since it consists only of words.

FALSITY OF HUMAN VIRTUES

When the Duke de la Rochefaucauld set down his thoughts on self-love and discovered man's driving force, a certain M. Esprit, an Oratorian, wrote a book called *Of the Falsity of Human Virtues*. According to M. Esprit, there is no virtue except by grace, and he ends each chapter by referring to Christian charity. Thus, according to M. Esprit, neither Cato nor Aristides nor Marcus Aurelius nor Epictetus was a good man. Good men can be found only among Christians. Among the Christians there is no virtue except among Catholics, and among Catholics the Jesuits, who are enemies of the Oratorians, must be excepted. It follows that virtue is scarcely found anywhere except among the enemies of the Jesuits.

This M. Esprit begins by stating that prudence is not a virtue, since it is often deceived. He might as well have said that Caesar was not a great captain because he was defeated at Dyrrachium.

If M. Esprit had been a philosopher, he would have considered prudence not as a virtue but as a talent—as a useful and happy quality; for even a rascal—and I have known many of them—can be prudent.

FANATICISM

Fanaticism is to superstition what delirium is to fever or rage to anger. One who experiences states of ecstasy and visions, and who mistakes dreams for reality or his own imaginings for prophecy is an enthusiast; one who is impelled by his enthusiasm to commit murder is a fanatic. . . . The most detestable example of fanaticism is that of the Parisians who on the night of Saint Bartholomew went about killing, butchering, hurling through the windows and tearing to pieces their fellow citizens who were not attending mass. Examples of cold-blooded fanatics are the judges who sentence to death men whose only crime is in not thinking as they themselves think. . . .

There is no remedy for this epidemical malady other than the philosophical attitude which by gradually winning adoption at last softens the manners of men, thereby preventing the access of the disease; for if the disease starts to spread, we must flee and wait for the air to be purified. Laws and religion will not protect us against spiritual pestilence; religion, far from being an effective antidote, turns into poison in diseased minds. . . . Only one of the world's religions has not been sullied by fanaticism, and that is the religion of the learned in China. The different sects of ancient philosophers were exempt from this pestilence; moreover, they provided the best possible antidote. The effect of philosophy is to calm the soul, and fanaticism and tranquillity are incompatible. That this infernal fury has so frequently polluted our own holy religion must be attributed to the fanaticism of mankind.

FASTING

Why did people first take it upon themselves to fast? Was it because their physicians prescribed fasting to relieve their indigestion, or did the fast days prescribed in melancholy religions originate in the lack of appetite experienced in grief? Did the Jews adopt the practice of fasting from the Egyptians, all of whose rites they imitated, including flagellation and the scapegoat...?

Foolish and cruel priests, for whom do you prescribe fasting? Is it for the rich? They are careful not to fast. Is it for the poor? They fast all during the year. The unhappy farmer scarcely ever eats meat, and he lacks the means to buy fish. Fools that you are, when will you amend your absurd laws?

FINAL CAUSES

It seems that only an idiot would deny that stomachs are made for digesting, eyes for seeing, and ears for hearing. But a man must have a strange predilection for final causes to assert that stone was made for building houses and that silkworms originated in China in order that we might wear satin in Europe. Against this, it might be argued that if God has obviously done one thing by design, then He has done all things by design. It is ridiculous to admit providence in one instance and deny it in others. Everything that is done was foreseen and prearranged. There is no arrangement without an object, no effect without a cause. It follows that everything is equally the result or the product of a final cause. It is just as true, therefore, to say that noses were made for wearing glasses and fingers for being adorned with diamonds as it is to say that ears were made for hearing sounds and eyes for receiving light.

I believe that this difficulty can easily be resolved. When effects are invariably the same in all places and times and when these uniform effects are independent of the beings to which they belong, then there is obviously a final cause.

FLOOD

Since the flood was the most miraculous event in the history of the world, to attempt to explain it would be absurd. Some mysteries must be accepted on faith; and faith consists in believing what reason denies, which is yet another miracle.

Thus the account of the universal flood is like that of the tower of Babel, Balaam's ass, the falling of the walls of Jericho at the sound of trumpets, water turned into blood, the crossing of the Red Sea, and all the other miracles which God deigned to perform for His chosen people. They are depths unfathomable to the human mind.

FRAUD

The fakir Bambabef once met one of the disciples of Confutzee (whom we call Confucius). Bambabef defended the necessity of deceiving people but the disciple, who was named Wang, asserted that no one should ever be deceived. Here we record the main points of their arguments:

BAMBABEF. We must imitate the Supreme Being. He does not show us things as they are. . . .

WANG. All men are alike. They are born with the same dispositions. Their nature is corrupted by the fakirs.

BAMBABEF. I admit that we teach them falsehood, but that is for their own good. We make them believe that if they fail to buy our blessed nails or to expiate their sins by giving us money, in the next life they will become post horses, dogs, or lizards. We intimidate them, and they become good people.

WANG. Don't you see that you are perverting these poor people? In their ranks are many more rational men than you think. They make fun of your miracles and superstition, and they see clearly that they will not be changed into lizards or post horses. And what is the result? They have enough good sense to see that you are preaching an absurd religion but not enough to aspire to a pure religion—one untrammeled by superstition—like ours. Their passions make them believe that there is no religion because the only one taught them is ridiculous. You become guilty of all the vices into which they plunge.

BAMBABEF. Not at all, for we teach them only good morals.

WANG. You would be stoned by the people if you taught them bad morals. The make-up of men is such that they enjoy doing evil but will not have it preached to them. The only thing is that good morals should not be adulterated by absurd fables. . . . Our literati are basically the same as our tailors, our weavers, and our laborers. They worship a god who is their creator and who rewards and punishes. Their worship is not sullied by absurd systems nor by extravagant cere-monies. . . . Some things are necessary to all. Everyone must be just, and the surest way of inspiring justice in all men is to inspire in them religion without superstition.

FREEDOM

B. But I ask you once more, am I not free?

A. Your will is not free, but your actions are. You are free to act when you have the power to act.

B. But all the books that I have read on the freedom of indif-ference—

A. Balderdash! There is no such thing as freedom of indifference. That is a phrase that makes no sense, invented by people who had almost none.

FREEDOM OF THOUGHT

Around 1707, after the English had won the battle of Saragossa, protected Portugal, and provided Spain with a king for some time, Lord Boldemind, an English general who had been wounded, was taking the baths in Barèges, where he met Count Medroso. . . .

BOLDEMIND. So you are a sergeant of the Dominicans. That is a wretched vocation.

MEDROSO. You are right. But I'd rather be their valet than their victim. And I chose the misfortune of burning my neighbor rather than being roasted myself.

BOLDEMIND. What a horrible alternative. You were a hundred times happier under the yoke of the Moors, who allowed you to wallow in your superstitions, and who, though victors, did not arrogate to themselves the exclusive right to shackle minds. . . . It is shameful to put your mind in the hands of those whom you would not entrust with your money. Dare to think for yourself.

MEDROSO. They say that if everyone thought for himself, confusion would result.

BOLDEMIND. Quite the contrary. . . . Those who have enslaved minds have caused a goodly part of the misfortunes of the world. We have known happiness in England only since we have had the right to speak our opinions freely.

MEDROSO. Everything is also quite calm in Lisbon where no one dares express an opinion.

BOLDEMIND. You are calm, but you are not happy. Yours is the calm of galley slaves who row in cadence and in silence.

MEDROSO. You believe, then, that my mind is in the galleys?

BOLDEMIND. Yes, and I would like to deliver it.

MEDROSO. But suppose I am content in the galleys?

BOLDEMIND. In that case, you deserve to be there.

FRIENDSHIP

Friendship is a tacit contract between two sensible and virtuous persons. I say sensible, for a monk or a celibate, though in no way wicked, may live without experiencing friendship. I say virtuous, for wicked men have only accomplices, revelers have only partners, businessmen have only associates, politicians assemble only factions, ordinary loafers have only companions, and princes have only courtesans; virtuous men alone have friends. Lethegus was Catelan's accomplice and Maecenas was Octavius' courtier, but Cicero was Atticus' friend. What sustains the contract between two tender, honest minds? The strength or weakness of its obligations varies according to the sensibility of the parties to the contract and the number of services rendered.

The Greeks and Arabs have shown more enthusiasm for friendship than we have. The tales which they have imagined on the subject of friendship command admiration; we have nothing to compare with them, for we are somewhat reserved in everything.

Friendship figured in the religion and legislation of the Greeks. The Thebans had a regiment of lovers—a fine regiment. Some have mistaken it for a regiment of sodomites. Their mistake was in judging a noble ideal by some of its accessory effects. Friendship among the Greeks was prescribed by law and religion. Manners countenanced perversion, but the law did not.

G

GENESIS

What can we say about Lot, who proposed to the people of Sodom that his two daughters be substituted for the two angels, and about his wife, who was changed into a pillar of salt, and about all the rest of the story? The ancient Arabian fable of Kinyras and Myrrha bears a resemblance to Lot's incest; and the adventure of Philemon and Baucis bears a resemblance to the appearance of angels to Lot and his wife. As for the pillar of salt, we are unable to cite a parallel, if not perhaps in the tale of Orpheus and Eurydice. . . .

Some eminent Fathers of the Church saw fit to adopt the practice of the Jews, and particularly of Philo, and to turn all these accounts into allegories. Some of the popes, even more discreet, tried to prevent the translation of these books into the vulgar language for fear that men might take it upon themselves to pass judgment on what they were supposed to worship.

We have every right to conclude that those who thoroughly understand this book ought to be tolerant toward those who, through no fault of their own, do not; but those who understand nothing ought also to be tolerant toward those who understand everything.

GLORY

"Miserable earthworms called men, what have you in common with the glory of the Supreme Being? Can He love glory? Can He receive it from you? Can He enjoy it? How long, two legged, featherless animals, will you fashion God in your own image? What! Because you are vain and love glory, would you have God love it also? If there were several gods, perhaps each of them would curry the favor of his equals. That might be a god's glory. Such a god, if infinite greatness and extreme lowliness are comparable, would be like King Alexander or Iscander, who saw fit to enter the lists with none but kings. But you poor creatures, what glory can you give to God? Stop profaning His sacred name. One emperor, Octavius Augustus, fearing that his name might be vilified, forbade his being praised in the schools of Rome. But you can neither vilify the Supreme Being nor honor Him. Humble yourselves, worship, and be silent."

Those were the words of Ben-al-betif. And the dervishes shouted, "Glory to God! Well spoken, Ben-al-betif."

GOD

During the reign of Arcadius, Logomachos, a canon in Constantinople, journeyed to Scythia and stopped at the foot of Mount Caucasus in the fertile plains of Zephirim on the border of Colchis. Dondindac, a good old man . . . was on his knees . . . singing the praises of God. "What are you doing there, idolater?" said Logomachos. "I am not an idolater," said Dondindac. "You must be," replied Logomachos, "for you are a Scythian, not a Greek. Let's see if you know your catechism. Why do you pray to God?"

DONDINDAC. Because it is right to worship the Supreme Being from whom we have everything.

LOGOMACHOS. Not bad for a barbarian. . . . Who told you that there is one God?

DONDINDAC. All nature tells me.

LOGOMACHOS. That is not enough. What is your conception of God?

DONDINDAC. He is my creator and my master. He will reward me if I am good and punish me if I am bad.

LOGOMACHOS. Trifles, mere trivialities. Let's get to the heart of the matter. Is God *infinite secundum quid,* or is He according to essence?

DONDINDAC. I don't understand you.

LOGOMACHOS. Stupid creature, is God in one place, beyond any place or in every place?

DONDINDAC. I have never thought about these things. . . . But let me ask you a question. I once saw one of your temples. Why do you show God with a long beard?

LOGOMACHOS. That is a very difficult question and one which requires preliminary instruction.

GOSPEL

None of the early Fathers of the Church cited a single passage from the four gospels that we accept today. . . .Our enemies note further that the very earliest Fathers of the Church not only failed to quote from the Gospels but they even referred to several passages found only in the apocryphal gospels rejected by the canon. . . . Our adversaries have concluded that since many false gospels were at first thought to be true, those which today constitute the foundation of our own faith may also have been forged. They place much emphasis on the faith of the first heretics who died for the apocryphal gospels. . . . The exacting Socinians refuse, therefore, to consider our four divine Gospels as anything other than clandestine works. The other Christians have as their only weapon against them the Holy Scripture, with the result that the two groups remain at odds but never come directly to grips.

GRACE

Holy councilors of modern Rome, illustrious and infallible theologians, no one has more respect than I for your divine decisions; but if Paulus Aemilius, Scipio, Cato, Cicero, Caesar, Titus, Trajan, or Marcus Aurelius returned to the city to which they once brought renown, you must confess that they would be somewhat astonished at your decisions on grace. What would they say if they heard you talking about physical grace according to St. Thomas and medicinal grace according to Cajetan, of inner and outer grace; of gratuitous, sanctifying, actual, habitual, incorporating grace; of efficacious grace which is sometimes ineffective; of sufficing grace, which is sometimes insufficient; and of versatile and congruous grace? Would they really comprehend it better than you and I. . . . ?

Why should the absolute master of the universe be more concerned with directing the interior of a single man than with governing the rest of nature in its entirety. . . . ? How pitiable to suppose that he is continually shaping, undoing, and reshaping our sentiments! And how audacious to think that we stand apart from all other beings! . . . Wretched man, behold the oak that rears its head to the clouds and the reed that bends at its feet. You do not say that efficacious grace was given to the oak and withheld from the reed. Lift up your eyes to the heavens and see the eternal Demiurge create millions of worlds which gravitate toward one another in accordance with all-encompassing and eternal law. . . . Do not repeat the folly of the foolish atom who said that the Eternal has particular laws for some atoms in your vicinity; that He bestows His grace on a certain individual and withholds it from another; that one who lacked grace yesterday shall have it tomorrow. God made the universe and He is not going to create new winds to sweep a few straws from one corner of His universe. Theologians are like the combatants in Homer who believed that the gods sometimes took up arms against them and sometimes sided with them. If Homer had not been considered a poet, he would have been charged with blasphemy.

H

HEAVEN OF THE ANCIENTS

If Homer had been asked to which heaven Sarpedon's soul had gone and where Hercules' soul resided, he would have been somewhat embarrassed and by way of reply, he would have improvised some harmonious lines. What assurance was there that the ethereal soul of Hercules would be more comfortable on Venus or on Saturn than on our globe? Could it have found repose on the sun? In view of the heat there this seems unlikely. Exactly what did the ancients mean by heaven? They were uncertain. They were always shouting, "Heaven and earth!" They might as well have shouted infinity and atom. There is really no such thing as heaven. There are a prodigious number of globes revolving in the immensity of space, and our globe revolves like the others.

The ancients thought that to go to heaven was to ascend, but from one globe to another there is no ascent. The heavenly bodies are sometimes above and sometimes below our horizon. If Venus should visit Paphos and then return to her own planet after it had set, she would not ascend in reference to our horizon but would descend. The proper expression would therefore be that she descended to heaven. But the ancients were not so discriminating; they had vague, uncertain, contradictory notions about everything pertaining to the physical world. Huge volumes have been written about their thinking on such questions. Four words would have been sufficient. They did not think.

We must always except a small number of sages, but they came too late. Few of them explained their thoughts, and when they did, the ruling charlatans sent them to heaven by the shortest route.

HELL

Even in primitive societies men must have realized that a number of criminals were escaping punishment. They punished public crimes, but they also had to find some means of checking secret crimes. This check was to be found only in religion. The Persians, Chaldeans, Egyptians, and Greeks all had the notion of punishment after this life. Of all the nations of antiquity known to us today, only the Jews believed in temporal punishment alone. . . .

Many of the Fathers of the Church did not believe in eternal punishment. To them it seemed absurd to burn a poor man throughout eternity for having stolen a goat. . . .

Not long ago, a good, well-meaning Huguenot minister preached and wrote that the damned would one day be pardoned, that there had to be a ratio between sin and suffering, and that a momentary transgression could not merit eternal punishment. This indulgent judge was deposed by his colleagues, one of whom said, "My friend, I don't believe in eternal punishment any more than you do, but it is good for your servant, your tailor, and even your lawyer to believe in it."

HISTORY OF THE JEWISH KINGS
AND OF THE PARALIPOMENA

Every nation, immediately after perfecting a system of writing, has written its own history. The Jews are no exception. Before they had kings, they lived under a theocracy; they were destined to be governed by God himself. . . .

Though the style of the history of the kings and of the paralipomena may be divine, it is still possible that the actions recounted in these histories are not. David murdered Uriah; Ishbosheth and Mephibosheth were murdered; Absalom murdered Ammon; Joab murdered Absalom; Solomon murdered his brother Adonijah; Baasha murdered Nadab; Zimri murdered Ela; Omri murdered Zimri; Ahab murdered Naboth; Jehu murdered Ahab and Joram; the inhabitants of Jerusalem murdered Amaziah, the son of Joash; Shallum, the son of Jabesh, murdered Zachariah, the son of Jeroboam; Menahem murdered Shallum, the son of Jabesh; Pekah, the son of Remaliah, murdered Pekahiah, the son of Menahem and Hoshea, the son of Ela, murdered Pekah, the son of Remaliah. Many lesser murders were passed over in silence. We must admit that if the Holy Spirit wrote this history, he did not choose a very edifying subject.

I

IDEA

Tatian, in his discourse to the Greeks, states that the soul is evidently composed of a body. Irenaeus, in the twenty-sixth chapter of his second book, states that the Lord taught that the soul preserved the shape of the body in order to retain its memory. Tertullian assures us in his second book on the soul that it is a body. Arnobius, Lactanius, Hilary, Gregory of Nyssa, and Ambrose are all of the same opinion. Some pretend that other Fathers of the Church maintain that the soul is without extension and that in this respect they are in agreement with Plato; this, however, is doubtful. I myself am reluctant to venture an opinion. I see nothing but incomprehensibility in either system; and after spending a lifetime meditating on the subject, I still stand exactly where I stood the first day. . . . It is saddening to have so many ideas and yet to have no precise knowledge concerning the nature of ideas.

That much I admit, but it is even more saddening and much more foolish for a man to believe that he knows what he does not know.

IDOL—IDOLATER—IDOLATRY

As long as they have existed, men—that is, weak animals, capable of reasoning and folly, subject to all accident, to sickness, and to death—have been aware of their weakness and their dependence. It has not been hard for them to posit the existence of something more powerful than they. . . . We do not know when men began to make for themselves idols, but we know that idols are of the greatest antiquity. . . . It is evident that priests attached as much divinity as they possibly could to their statues in order to attract more offerings. We know that philosophers inveighed against these superstitions, that warriors made fun of them, that magistrates tolerated them, and that the people, always absurd, never knew what they were doing. That, in a word, is the history of all nations to which God has not revealed himself. . . .

Among all the nations of so-called idolaters, there were sacred theology and profane error, secret worship and public ceremonies, the religion of the sages and the religion of the common people. The mysteries taught the existence of but one god. Typical of all the Eleusinian mysteries, renowned throughout Europe and Asia, is the hymn attributed to the ancient Orpheus: "Contemplate divine nature, illuminate thy spirit, govern thy heart, walk in the path of righteousness; let the God of heaven and earth be always present to thine eyes. He is unique. He alone exists independently; all beings derive from Him their essence; He sustains them all; He has never been seen by mortals and He sees all things."

Or we may turn to this passage written by the philosopher Maximus, whom we have previously quoted: "What man is so uncouth and so stupid as to doubt that there is a supreme, eternal, and infinite god who has engendered nothing like himself and who is the common father of all things?"

There are a thousand indications that the sages abhorred not only idolatry but also polytheism. . . . The Stoics and Platonists believed in a divine and universal nature; the Epicureans did not. The pontiffs spoke of but one God in their mysteries. Where, then, were the idolaters?

INQUISITION

The Inquisition, as everybody knows, is an admirable and truly Christian invention to increase the power of the Pope and monks, and to turn the population of a whole kingdom into hypocrites. . . . The animal skins in which God clothed Adam and Eve were the model for the *san benito* which the holy office requires heretics to wear. The same line of reasoning, of course, can be used to prove not only that God was the first tailor, but also that He was the first inquisitor.

Adam was deprived of all his real property in the terrestrial paradise; this explains why the Holy Office confiscates the goods of all those whom it condemns. . . .

Men are imprisoned on the basis of accusations made by the most infamous persons. A son can denounce his father or a woman her husband. Never is the accused confronted by his accusers, and property is confiscated for the benefit of the judges—that, at least, is how the Inquisition has been functioning until the present. That men should patiently have endured this yoke is incomprehensible.

J

JEPHTHAH OR HUMAN SACRIFICES

It is evident from the text of the Book of Judges that Jephthah promised to sacrifice the first person who came out of his house to congratulate him on his victory over the Ammonites. His only daughter came before him for that purpose. He rent his garments and immolated her after allowing her to go into the mountains to deplore her misfortune in dying a virgin. The daughters of Israel continued for a long time to celebrate this episode, devoting four days each year to grieving for Jephthah's daughter. . . .

The Jewish law stipulated that men devoted to the Lord should be put to death. . . . It was by virtue of this law that Samuel mutilated the body of King Agag. . . . The Jews, then, did sacrifice human beings. No point in history is better documented. We can judge a nation only through its own archives and through its account of its own history.

JOB

Good day, friend Job! You are one of the oldest characters mentioned in Scripture. You were not a Jew. We know that

the book which bears your name is older than the Pentateuch.
. . . You lived in Chaldea. Worthy commentators pretend that
you believed in the Resurrection because, prostrate on your
dunghill, you said (Chapter 14) that you would one day rise
up from it. A patient concerned with his recovery is not
anxious to be resurrected, but I want to talk to you about
other things.

You were a great braggart, but your friends were even
more boastful. They said that you owned seven thousand
sheep, three thousand camels, one thousand cows. . . . I have
been much richer than you; and although I have lost much
of my property and am ill like you, I have not murmured
against God as your friends seem to accuse you of having
done.

I am not at all pleased with Satan who, to induce you to
sin and to make you forget God, asked to be allowed to
take from you all your property and to give you the itch.
It is in such a state that men always have recourse to the
Divinity. Those who are happy forget Him. Satan did not
know enough about the world at that time; since then, he
has learned.

JOSEPH

The Book of Joseph, considered simply as an object of
curiosity and as a piece of literature, is one of the most
precious monuments bequeathed to us by antiquity. It seems
to be the model of all the Oriental writers. It has greater
emotional impact than Homer's Odyssey; for a hero who
forgives is more touching than one who seeks revenge.

We look upon the Arabs as the first authors of these

ingenious fictions which have found their way into every language, but I find among them no tale comparable to that of Joseph. Almost everything about it commands admiration, and the end can provoke a flood of tears. . . . We find in this story everything that makes for an interesting epic poem—exposition, plot, recognition, catastrophe, and the marvelous. Nothing bears more plainly the stamp of Oriental genius.

The answer which the good man Jacob, Joseph's father, gave to Pharaoh ought to impress all those who can read. "How old are you?" asked the king. "I am one hundred and thirty years old," said the old man, "and I have not yet known one happy day during my short pilgrimage."

JUDEA

I have never been to Judea, thank God, and I never will go there. I have seen people from every land who have come back from there; they have all told me that the situation in Jerusalem is horrible; that all the land in the vicinity is stony; that the mountains are bare; that the famous River Jordan is not more than forty-five feet wide; that the only good part of the country is Jericho; in short, all of them say the same thing as St. Jerome, who lived for such a long time in Bethlehem and who described the country as Nature's dump. He said that in summer there was not even water to drink. Yet this land must have seemed luxuriant and delightful to the Jews in contrast to the desert lands from which they had originally come. . . . If God was leading the Jews and wanted to give them good land, and if these wretched people were actually living in Egypt, why did He not allow them to remain there? Instead of an answer, we hear theological recitals.

JULIAN

Justice is often delayed. Two or three writers, either mercenaries or fanatics, deified the barbarous and effeminate Constantine and treated as a miscreant the just, wise, and great Julian. All other writers, copying them, repeated both their flattery and their calumny. These misconceptions became almost an article of faith. Finally the age of sound criticism arrived and after fourteen hundred years, enlightened men reviewed the judgment of the ignorant. Constantine was revealed as an opportunist who scoffed at God and men. He had the insolence to pretend that God had placed in the heavens a sign assuring him of victory. He bathed in the blood of all his relatives and fell asleep in the lap of luxury, but he was a Christian and was canonized.

Julian was sober, chaste, disinterested, brave, and merciful. But he was not a Christian and was for a long time regarded as a monster.

Today, having studied the documents, records, and reports relating to Julian and his enemies, we are compelled to acknowledge that if he had no love for Christianity, he at least had good reason to hate a sect stained with the blood of all his family. . . . In short, an impartial investigation of the facts obliges us to admit that Julian had all of Trajan's qualities except the vice long condoned among the Greeks and Romans; all of Cato's virtues, but not his stubbornness or ill humor; all of Julius Caesar's admirable qualities, but none of his vices; and he had Scipio's continence. In short he was in every respect equal to Marcus Aurelius, the greatest of men.

L

LAW (CIVIL AND ECCLESIASTICAL)

Among the papers of a lawyer were found these notes, which may merit some consideration. . . . Everything relating to marriages ought to depend solely on the magistrate and priests should have charge of the august function of blessing them. . . . No priest should ever have the authority to deprive a citizen of even the smallest of his privileges under the pretext that the citizen is a sinner; the priest, who is himself a sinner, ought to pray for sinners, not judge them.

Magistrates, husbandmen, and priests alike should contribute to the expenses of the state, for all are its subjects.

There should be but one system of weights, measures, and usages.

The punishment of criminals should serve a purpose. A hanged man is good for nothing; a man who is sentenced to perform public services, however, serves his country and is at the same time an object lesson.

Every law should be clear, uniform, and exact; for to interpret a law is almost always to corrupt it.

Nothing but vice should be held infamous.

Taxes always should be in just proportions.

Law never should contradict usage; for if usage is good, law is worthless.

LAWS

My neighbor was brought to ruin by a lawsuit over two oaks which belonged to him. The trees that he had had chopped down were in his own forest, but he had failed to observe a certain technicality with which he could scarcely have been acquainted. His wife died in poverty and his son is eking out a wretched existence. I admit that these laws are just, even though their execution is somewhat harsh. But I cannot condone laws which authorize a hundred thousand men loyally to cut their neighbors' throats. It would seem to me that most men have received from nature enough common sense to make laws, but that nowhere in the whole world is there sufficient justice to make good laws. . . .

To the disgrace of mankind, as we all know, gaming rules are the only laws that are consistently just, clear, inviolable, and susceptible of execution. Why is the Indian who formulated the laws for playing chess willingly obeyed anywhere in the world while papal decrees, for example, are today regarded with horror and contempt? It is because the inventor of chess devised a set of rules to satisfy players but popes in their decrees sought only what would be to their own advantage. The Indian tried both to stimulate and to relax men's minds; the popes were desirous of debasing them.

LETTERS (MEN OF)

The men of letters who have rendered the greatest services to the small number of sentient beings scattered throughout the world are the isolated sages, true scholars locked in their rooms, who have neither publicly debated in the universities nor spoken half-truths in the academies; and almost all of them have been persecuted. Our wretched species is so created that those who tread the beaten path always cast stones at those who would show them a new one. . . .

To incur the jealousy of his colleagues, to be the victim of cabals, to be held in contempt by men in high places—none of these is the greatest misfortune of a man of letters; it is rather to be judged by fools. Fools sometimes go very far, especially when fanaticism is joined to incompetence, and incompetence to a spirit of vengeance. Another great misfortune is that the man of letters generally has nothing for support. The average citizen buys a small business and finds support among his fellow citizens. If someone wrongs him in some way, he soon finds defenders. The man of letters is helpless. He is like a flying fish. If he rises too high, the birds will devour him. If he goes down too far, the fish will eat him.

LOVE

If you wish to understand what love is, look at the sparrow in your garden. Look at the doves. Contemplate the bull as he is led to the heifer. Behold the proud horse as he is led by his caretakers to the waiting mare. . . . But discount jealousy and think what advantages over the animals are possessed by the human species. Human love compensates for all those advantages given by nature to animals—such as strength, beauty, lightness, and swiftness. . . . No animal other than man can embrace . . . or surrender himself at all seasons to the endearments of love. If you consider these important points, you will say along with the Earl of Rochester, "Love would make a nation of atheists worship the Divinity."

Endowed with the gift of perfecting whatever they are given by nature, men have achieved perfect love. . . . All the other sentiments later intermingle with that of love, just as metals amalgamate with gold. Friendship and esteem fortify love, while physical and mental attributes forge still other bonds. . . . Such are the advantages enjoyed by man; but if he experiences delights unknown to animals, he is also exposed to many vexations from which they are free. The most dreadful of all is occasioned by the fact that nature has used a terrible disease to which man alone is subject to poison the pleasures of love and sources of life of three-fourths of the world. . . . Can this, then, be the best of all possible worlds? If Caesar and Antony and Octavius never had the disease, did it have to cause the death of Francis I? Yes, it is said. Things were so ordered for the best. Though I try, I find this hard to believe.

LUXURY

People have spoken against luxury for the last two thousand years in verse and in prose, and yet they have always liked it. Much has been said in defense of the Romans. We are told that these robbers were disinterested and virtuous men when they ravaged and plundered their neighbors' harvests and when, to build up their own wretched village, they destroyed those of the Volsci and Samnites. The fact is that they were as yet unable to steal either gold or silver or precious stones because there were none in the towns that they sacked and plundered. Their forests and their swamps produced neither partridges nor pheasants, and yet people praised them for their temperance.

After they had finally pillaged and plundered everything from the Adriatic Sea to the Euphrates and had sense enough to enjoy the fruit of their rapine; when they began to cultivate all the arts, to taste all the pleasures of life, and even to communicate them to the nations they had conquered, then they ceased, we are told, to be wise and upright.

All these statements simply prove that a thief ought never to eat the dinner that he has stolen, nor wear the garment that he has taken, nor put on a ring that he has pillaged. He ought, rather, it is said, to throw everything into the river and live like an upright person; what we really ought to condemn is the original act. We should condemn bandits when they pillage but refrain from treating them as madmen for reveling in the spoils.

M

MADNESS

Madness is a disease of the brain, which necessarily prevents a man from thinking and acting like other men. If he is unable to manage his property, it is taken from his hands; if he is unable to entertain ideas acceptable to society, he is excluded from it; if he is dangerous, he is put in confinement; if he is insane, he is put in a strait jacket.

It is important to observe, however, that this madman is not deprived of ideas. He has just as many as other men during his waking hours, and often when he sleeps. Why is it that the immortal mind lodged in his brain receives distinct and accurate impressions through the senses, yet lacks the capacity for sound judgment. . . ?

The faculty of thought bestowed upon man by God is subject, like the other senses, to derangement. Madness is a disease of the brain, just as goutiness is a disease of the feet and hands. People use their brains to think and their feet to walk, yet know nothing of the source of either the incomprehensible power of walking or the equally incomprehensible power of thinking.

MARTYRS

We have had enough false martyrs foisted upon us to provide laughter. The Tituses, Trajans, and Marcus Aureliuses, all models of virtue, are depicted as monsters of cruelty. Flury, a priest in Loc-Dieu, has polluted his ecclesiastical history by relating tales which a sensible woman would not tell to little children. . . .

Do you wish good, well-authenticated accounts of barbarities—well-documented accounts of massacres, of rivers of blood which have actually flowed, of fathers and mothers and husbands and wives and suckling children who actually have had their throats cut and have been piled one on another? Persecuting monsters, you will find these truths in your own records—in the crusades against the Albigenses, in the massacres at Merindol and Cabrière, in the terrible day of St. Bartholomew, in the massacres in Ireland and in the valleys of the canton of Vaud. It is only fitting for you barbarians that you are to impute to the best of emperors extravagant cruelties—you who have bathed Europe in blood and covered it with corpses to prove that the same body can be in a thousand places at the same time and that the pope can sell indulgences! Heap calumny no longer on the Romans, you lawgivers, but instead ask God to forgive you for the abominations of your forefathers!

MASTER

How did one man ever manage to become the master of another? And by what sort of incomprehensible magic did he ever manage to become the master of several other men?

75

A great number of good volumes have been written on this subject. . . . I do not know what happened in the order of time, but in that of nature, we must agree that men are born equal and that violence and ability made the first masters. The present ones have been made by laws.

MATTER

Wise men, when asked what the soul is, reply that they do not know. If they are asked what matter is, they give the same reply. It is true that certain professors, especially unseasoned professors, know all about matter. When they have said that matter is measurable and divisible, they think that they have said everything; but when they are asked to state what this thing is, they are embarrassed. "It is made up of parts," they say. "And these parts, of what are they composed?" Then they fall silent, or they become very loquacious, which is equally suspicious. . . . An explanation of the eternity of matter, like all other explanations, poses great difficulties. A system that explains the formation of matter out of nothing is no less incomprehensible. We must simply accept the facts and not pretend to account for them. Philosophy cannot explain everything. . . .

Fortunately, none of the systems that we might adopt will corrupt our morals. Whether matter is created or shaped is of no great importance. God is still our absolute master. It behooves us to be virtuous on a chaotic world reduced to order or on a chaotic world created out of nothing. Few of these metaphysical questions affect the conduct of life. Such disputes resemble table talk: each of us forgets after dinner what he has said and is guided by his own inclination and taste.

MESSIAH

Everyone knows that the Jews, with their literal minds, have never penetrated the meaning of the Scriptures as we have.

When the Saviour appeared, the prejudiced Jews rose up against Him. Jesus Christ himself, to avoid upsetting them in their blindness, seems to have been extremely reserved on the subject of His divinity. "He wished," said St. Chrysostom, "imperceptibly to accustom his auditors to believing a mystery far above their understanding." By assuming God's authority and pardoning sin, he incited all those who witnessed the act. His most striking miracles could not convince even those for whom he performed them of his divinity. When before the Sanhedrin he acknowledged by a modest hint that he was the son of God, the high priest tore his robe and shouted, "Blasphemy!" Before the sending of the Holy Ghost, the apostles did not even suspect their master's divinity. When He asked them what the people thought of Him, they replied that some took Him for Elias, others for Jeremiah or some other prophet. A particular revelation was necessary to make known to St. Peter that Jesus was the Christ, the son of the living God.

The Jews revolted against the divinity of Jesus Christ and had recourse to all sorts of expedients to destroy the great mystery. They distorted the meaning of their own oracles or did not apply them to the Messiah. . . . They maintained that if the Saviour and after him the evangelists, the apostles, and the first Christians called Jesus the son of God, in evangelical times this august term merely signified the opposite of son of Belial—that is, an upright man, a servant of God, in contrast to a wicked man without fear of the Lord.

METAMORPHOSIS AND METEMPSYCHOSIS

It is not in the least surprising that all the metamorphoses observed throughout the world should have made the Orientals, who have imagined everything, imagine that our souls pass from one body to another. An almost imperceptible dot becomes a caterpillar, and this caterpillar becomes a butterfly; an acorn is transformed into an oak, an egg into a bird; water becomes a cloud and thunder; wood changes to fire and ashes; everything in nature, in short, seems to undergo metamorphosis. The Orientals attributed to human souls, which were regarded as almost imperceptible shapes, the characteristics observable in less ethereal bodies. The idea of metempsychosis is perhaps the most ancient dogma of the known universe and is still prevalent in a great part of India and China. It is also quite probable that the various metamorphoses which we observe produced the ancient fables that Ovid collected in his admirable work. Even the Jews have their metamorphoses. Niobe was changed into stone, and Edith, Lot's wife, into a pillar of salt. Eurydice was kept in the underworld because she looked backward, and it was for the same indiscretion that Lot's wife was deprived of her human nature. The town in which Baucis and Philemon lived in Phrygia was changed into a lake; the same thing happened to Sodom. The daughters of Anius changed water into oil; we have in Scripture a metamorphosis which is quite similar and which is more true and more sacred. Cadmus was changed into a serpent; Aaron's rod also became a serpent.

MIND (LIMITS OF THE HUMAN)

Questions about mind are everywhere, poor Doctor. Why do your arms and feet obey your will, while your liver does not? How does thought take shape in your fragile brain. . . . ? What is matter? Your peers have written ten thousand volumes on this subject. All they have found are a few of its qualities, which children know as well as you. But what, in reality, is this substance, and what is this thing that we, unable to name more precisely because of our ignorance, call spirit, from the Latin word meaning breath?

Study this weed that I cast on the ground and tell me how it springs up and produces a stalk laden with grain. Tell me how the same soil produces apples on one tree and chestnuts on another. My questions would fill a volume, and your answers would always be limited to five words: "I know nothing about it." And still you have received your degrees, your head is filled with facts, and you are called professor. And the conceited imbecile who boasts of a petty position in a petty town thinks that he has purchased the right to judge and to condemn that which he does not understand. Montaigne's motto was, "What do I know?" And yours should be, "What do I not know?"

MIRACLES

A miracle, according to the literal meaning of the word, is something admirable. In this sense, everything is a miracle. The prodigious order of nature, the rotation of a hundred million worlds around a million suns, the action of light, animal life, all are perpetual miracles.

Traditionally, we call a violation of these divine and eternal laws a miracle. A solar eclipse when the moon is full or a dead man who walks two leagues and carries his head in his arms, these we call miracles.

Several scientists hold that in this sense there are no miracles. They argue that a miracle is the violation of mathematical, divine, immutable, eternal laws. But inherent in their definition of a miracle is a contradiction in terms: A law cannot be immutable and at the same time violable. But when asked whether a law established by God himself can be suspended by its author, they have the termerity to reply that it cannot, and that an infinitely wise Being could not have made laws only to violate them. He could interfere with the machine, they say, only with a view to making it work better. But it is evident that God, omnipotent and omniscient, originally made this immense machine as good and perfect as He could. He provided in the beginning for any imperfections that might arise from the nature of matter and will therefore never change it in any way.

Furthermore, God can do nothing without a reason. What reason could he have for disfiguring for a time His own creation?

They are told that this is done in favor of certain men. They answer that He must act in favor of all men, since it is impossible to believe that divine nature would work for only a few special men and not for the whole human race; and even the whole human race is of no great importance, for it is less than a small ant hill in comparison with all the bodies that fill the vast universe. The height of folly is to imagine that the infinite Being would intervene in the eternal operation of the vast machinery that moves the whole universe in favor of three or four hundred ants on this little heap of dirt.

MORALITY

I have just read these words in a fourteen-volume declamation entitled *The History of the Lower Empire*: "The

Christians had a code of ethics, but the pagans had none."

Oh, M. LeBeau! You wrote these fourteen volumes. Where did you acquire such nonsense? What about the ethics of Socrates, of Zaleucus, of Charondas, of Cicero, of Epictetus, and of Marcus Aurelius?

There is but one code of ethics, M. LeBeau, as there is but one system of geometry. But you will tell me that most men know nothing about geometry. Yes, but after a little study, all men draw the same conclusions. Farmers, workmen, artists have not taken courses in ethics; they have read neither Cicero's *De Finibus* nor Aristotle's *Ethics;* but as soon as they begin to think, they are unwittingly disciples of Cicero. The Indian dyer, the Tartar shepherd, and the English sailor know about justice and injustice. Confucius did not invent a system of morals as men build physical systems. He found it in the hearts of all men. . . .

Morality is not to be found in superstition nor in ceremonies; it has nothing in common with dogmas. We cannot repeat too often that dogmas are different and that morality is the same among all men who make use of their reason. Morality proceeds, like light, from God; our superstitions are but darkness. Think it over, reader; enlarge upon this truth and draw your own consequences.

MOSES

Numerous scholars have held that the Pentateuch could not have been written by Moses. . . . But we are told that the ways of God are not the ways of men; that God has tested, led, and abandoned His people through a wisdom unknown to us; that for more than two thousand years the

Jews themselves have believed that Moses wrote these books; that the Church, which has succeeded the synagogue and which is equally infallible, has ruled on this point of controversy; and that scholars ought to be silent when the Church speaks.

N

NECESSITY

OSMIN. Don't you hold that everything is necessary?

SELIM. If not, it follows that God does useless things. . . .

OSMIN. Are some notions common to all men and necessary for the well-being of society?

SELIM. Yes. I have traveled with Paul Lucas, and wherever I went I saw that men respected their parents, that they felt obliged to keep their word, that they pitied oppressed innocence, that they detested persecution, that they looked upon freedom of thought as a natural right and on the enemies of this freedom as the enemies of mankind. Those who thought differently seemed to me to be badly organized creatures, as monstrous as those born without eyes or hands.

OSMIN. These necessary things, are they necessary in all times and in all places?

SELIM. Yes, otherwise they would not be necessary to the human race.

OSMIN. A new creed is therefore not necessary to this race. Men might very well have lived in society and carried out their duties toward God before they believed that Mohammed held frequent conversations with the angel Gabriel.

SELIM. Nothing is more obvious. . . . It follows that the Mohammedan religion cannot be a basic necessity to man.

OSMIN. But since it exists, has God permitted it?

SELIM. Yes, as he permits the world to abound in foolishness, errors, and calamities. This does not mean that men are all created to be essentially foolish and unhappy. God allows some men to be eaten by serpents, but it cannot be said that He created man to be eaten by serpents. . . .

OSMIN. I would have reason to complain about a physician who gave me a lecture on poisonous plants but neglected to point out to me a single one that was healthful.

SELIM. I'm not a physician and you're not a patient, but it seems to me that I'd be giving you a very good prescription if I told you to distrust all the fabrications of charlatans, to worship God, to be an honest man, and to believe that two and two are four.

O

OFFENSES (LOCAL)

Travel throughout the earth and you will find that theft, murder, adultery, and calumny are looked upon as offenses which society condemns and represses; but should something that is accepted in England and condemned in Italy be punished in Italy as if it were a crime against mankind? If something is criminal only within the confines of certain mountain ranges or between two rivers, should it not be judged less severely than outrages regarded with horror in all countries? Shouldn't the judge say to himself, "I wouldn't dare to punish in Ragusa what I punish in Loretto?"

OPTIMISM

"God," says Pope, "beholds with an equal eye a hero perish or a sparrow fall; the destruction of an atom, or the ruin of a thousand planets; the bursting of a bubble, or the dissolution of a world."

That, I must confess, is a pleasant consolation. And we can all take comfort in the statement of Lord Shaftesbury, who says that God will not derange his general system for so wretched an animal as man. But we must acknowledge at the very least that this pitiful creature has a right to cry out humbly and to seek to understand in his grief why God's eternal laws do not guarantee the well-being of every individual. The system of "Whatever is, is right," represents the Author of Nature as a powerful, malevolent monarch who shows no concern over the destruction of four or five hundred thousand men, or for multitudes of others who pass their days in penury and tears, provided that he succeeds in his designs.

The doctrine that this is the best of all possible worlds is anything but consolatory. The philosophers who embrace it are left without hope; for those who seek in good faith to fathom it, the question of good and evil is rooted in chaos. It is an intellectual exercise for disputants—prisoners playing with their chains. Those who do not concern themselves with the question are like fish that are transported from a river to a reservoir; they never suspect that they are there to be eaten during Lent. We ourselves know absolutely nothing about the forces that govern our destiny.

ORIGINAL SIN

The Socinians or Unitarians make capital of the doctrine of original sin. They call the acceptance of this doctrine the "original sin" of Christianity. It is an outrage against God, they say. To dare to say that He created all the successive generations of mankind only to subject them to eternal punishment under the pretext that their earliest ancestor ate of a particular fruit in a garden is to accuse him of the most absurd barbarity. This sacrilegious imputation is even more inexcusable among Christians, since there is no mention of this invention of original sin either in the Pentateuch or in the gospels, whether apocryphal or canonical, or in any of the writers called the "first Fathers of the Church." . . .

"What an abomination," exclaim the staunch Unitarians, "to slander the Creator by attributing to him perpetual miracles in order that he may damn eternal men whom he brings to birth for such a short span!" Souls were either created from all eternity, with the result that they are infinitely older than Adam's sin and have no connection with it, or they are formed at the time of conception, with the result that God must exercise eternal vigilance and create in each instance a new spirit that He will render eternally miserable, or God is Himself the soul of all mankind, with the result that He is damned along with His system. . . . I have merely reported the view of the Unitarians; but men have become so superstitious that I could hardly report it without trembling.

P

PAUL

What is meant by the ascension of Paul to the third heaven? What is the third heaven?

Which seems more likely (humanly speaking), that Paul became a Christian because he was knocked off his horse by the appearance of a great light at high noon and because a celestial voice cried out, "Saul, Saul, why persecuteth thou me?" or that he was angered by the Pharisees, either by Gamaliel's refusing to give him his daughter or for some other reason?

If the circumstances were different—if we were not obliged to believe in this miracle—Gamaliel's refusal would seem more natural than a celestial voice.

My only purpose in asking these questions is to be instructed; and I request anyone willing to instruct me to speak reasonably.

PERSECUTION

What is a persecutor? He whose wounded pride and unbridled fanaticism turn princes and magistrates against innocent men whose only crime is that of holding a different opinion. . . . When the persecution of the French Protestants began, it was neither Francis I nor Henry II nor Francis II who spied upon these unfortunate people, who vented upon them their studied fury, and who cast them into the flames in a spirit of vengeance. Francis I was too preoccupied with the Duchess d'Étampes; Henry II was giving too much attention to his jaded Diane; and Francis II was behaving too childishly. Who started these persecutions? Jealous priests who took advantage of the prejudices of magistrates and the political ambitions of ministers.

If these monarchs had not been deceived, if they had foreseen that the persecutions would lead to fifty years of civil wars and that one-half of the nation would exterminate the other, they would have extinguished with their tears the fire of the first stakes that they allowed to be ignited. Oh, God of mercy! If any man resembles the evildoer who is described as being forever engaged in destroying your works, isn't it the persecutor?

PETER

Why have Peter's successors had so much power in the West and none in the East? This is the same as asking why the bishops of Würzburg and Salzburg arrogated to themselves regal prerogatives in times of anarchy but the Greek bishops always remained subjects. Time, opportunity, the ambition of some and the weakness of others have done and will do everything in this world.

A famous German Lutheran (it was, I believe, Melanchthon) took exception to the notion that Jesus had said to Simon Barjonas, Sepha, or Sephas, "Thou art Peter, and upon this rock I will build my church." He could not believe that God would resort to such a play on words and that the power of the pope could have been founded on a pun. Peter was reputed to have been Bishop of Rome, but it is well known that there was no particular bishop then and for a long time thereafter. The society of Christians did not assume a regular form until near the end of the second century. It is possible that Peter went to Rome, and even that he was crucified with his head downward, though this was not the usual practice; but we have absolutely no proof of all this. . . .

A clergyman was once made to pay extortionately for a benefice at Rome—an offense known as simony. When asked some time afterward whether he thought Simon Peter had ever been in that city, he replied, "I don't think that Peter was ever there, but I am sure Simon was."

PHILOSOPHER

Philosopher means lover of wisdom, that is, of truth. All philosophers have had this twofold character. All the philosophers of antiquity gave to mankind examples of virtue and lessons in moral truths. All of them may well have been wrong about physics, but they knew all that was necessary for their conduct in life. Centuries were required to discover a part of the laws of nature. One day is all that is required for a sage to become acquainted with the duties of man.

The philosopher is not an enthusiast; he does not set himself up as a prophet; he does not claim to be inspired by the gods. . . . By what quirk of fate, disgraceful perhaps to western nations, do we have to go to the Far East to find a simple, unassuming sage who was teaching men how to live happily six hundred years before our vulgar era. . . . ? This sage was Confucius, who sought in his capacity as a lawgiver never to deceive mankind. What better rule of conduct has been given since his time anywhere in the world (rule a state as you rule a family; a man can govern his family only by setting a good example. . . .) A great number of Greek philosophers later taught an equally pure system of ethics. If they had limited themselves to their vain systems of physics, their names would be mentioned today only in derision. They are still respected because they taught other men to be just. . . . Where can we find a citizen who, like Julian, Antoninus, and Marcus Aurelius, would deprive himself of all the comforts of our luxurious and effeminate way of living? Who would sleep as they on the bare ground? Who would adopt their frugal practices. . . . We have our converts, but where are our sages? Where are those whose souls are unshakable, just, and tolerant? There have been some consecrated philosophers in France and all of them except Montaigne have been persecuted. . . . They have always been persecuted by fanatics. Is it actually possible for men of letters to engage in such persecution? For them to turn against their brothers the very weapons by which they are in turn wounded? Unhappy men of letters, must you serve as informers. . . . ?

How contemptible is a hypocrite! How abominable is a studied hypocrite! There were none in ancient Rome, which numbered a few men of letters among its many subjects. There were impostors, I admit, but not religious hypocrites, who are the most cowardly and cruel species of all. Why do we find no religious hypocrites in England, and why are there still so many in France? Philosophers, it will be easy for you to solve this problem.

POPERY

PAPIST. His Holiness has in his principalities Lutherans, Calvinists, Quakers, Anabaptists, and even Jews; and you would also have him admit Unitarians.

TREASURER. If these Unitarians bring in wealth and industry, how will they harm us? Your salary can only be increased.

PAPIST. I confess that the lowering of my salary would be more disagreeable to me than the admission of these people, but they don't believe that Jesus Christ is the son of God.

TREASURER. What does that matter to you, so long as you are allowed to believe it and are well fed, well dressed, and well lodged? The Jews are far from believing that he is the son of God, and yet you are glad to find here Jews with whom you can deposit your money at six per cent. St. Paul himself never spoke of the divinity of Jesus Christ, whom he candidly called a man. . . . All the early Fathers of the Church thought like Paul. It is obvious that Jesus was content with his humanity for three hundred years; picture yourself as a Christian during those times.

PAPIST. But sir, they refuse to believe in eternal punishment.

TREASURER. And so do I. Be damned forever if you wish, but I want no part of it.

PAPIST. Oh, sir, how hard it is not to be able to damn at will all the heretics in the world.

PREJUDICE

Prejudice is an opinion without judgment. Thus, people in every land, before their children are capable of exercising judgment, instill in them all desirable opinions.

Some universal and necessary prejudices are the epitome of virtue. In every land children are taught to acknowledge a god who rewards and punishes; to respect and love their father and mother; and to regard theft as a crime and a calculated lie as a vice before they can distinguish virtues from vices. . . .

If your nurse has told you that Ceres presides over wheat, or that *Vishnu Xaca* became a man several times, or that Sammonocodom chopped down a forest, or that Odin awaits you in his hall near Jutland, or that Mohammed or someone else traveled to heaven; and if your tutor later reinforces what your nurse has engraved on your brain, you will possess it for life. If your judgment seeks to overcome these prejudices, your neighbors, especially the ladies, charge you with blasphemy and frighten you; your dervish, fearing the termination of his revenue, denounces you to the cadi; and the cadi has you impaled if he can because he wants to command fools and believes that they are more obedient than others. These conditions will prevail until your neighbors and the dervish and the cadi begin to understand that folly is futile and that persecution is abominable.

PRIDE

Cicero in one of his letters says familiarly to his friend, "Send me the persons to whom you wish me to give the Gauls." In another letter he pretends to tire of letters from one prince after another thanking him for transforming their provinces into kingdoms, and he adds that he does not even know the location of these kingdoms.

It is possible that Cicero, who had often seen the Roman people—the sovereign people—applaud and obey him, and who was thanked by kings with whom he was acquainted, was no stranger to pride and vanity.

Though this sentiment hardly befits so wretched a creature as man, it can be condoned in a Cicero or a Caesar or a Scipio; but when in the heart of one of our half-barbarous provinces a man who may have bought a petty position and printed some mediocre lines gives himself over to pride, he becomes an object of ridicule.

PRIESTS

Priests in a state are like tutors in private families: their function is to teach, pray, and set examples. They ought to have no authority over the masters of the house unless it can be proved that the wage giver ought to obey the recipient. Of all religions, the one that most positively excludes priests from exercising any civil authority is assuredly that of Jesus: "Render unto Caesar the things that are Caesar's." "Among you there is neither first nor last." "My kingdom is not of this world."

The struggles between empires and the priesthood, which have bathed Europe in blood for more than six centuries, have been nothing more than rebellions on the part of priests against both God and man and a continuing sin against the Holy Ghost.

From Calchas, who assassinated Agamemnon's daughter, until Gregory XII and Sixtus V, two bishops of Rome who tried to wrest from the great Henry IV the kingdom of France, sacerdotal power has been fatal to the world.

PROPHETS

The prophet Jurieu was hissed, the prophets of the Cévennes were hanged or racked, the prophets who came from

Languedoc and Dauphiny to London were pilloried, the Anabaptist prophets were condemned to various tortures, the prophet Savonarola was burned in Florence, and the prophet John the Baptist was beheaded. . . .

The Jews were able to exalt their souls and see clearly all future events, but it is difficult to decide precisely whether by Jerusalem the prophets always mean eternal life; whether Babylon signifies London or Paris; whether when they speak of a great banquet they really mean a fast; whether red wine signifies blood; whether a red mantle signifies faith and a white one charity. To understand the prophets taxes the human mind. That is why I shall say no more.

R

RELIGION

Fourth question: once a religion is established in a state, the tribunals all function mainly to prevent the continuance or renewal of most of the things done in that religion before it won general acceptance. Its founders were accustomed to meet in secret against the will of magistrates. Now only public meetings approved by the law are permitted, and all concealed associations not authorized by law are forbidden. According to the old rule, it was better to obey God than man. Now the accepted rule is the reverse, namely, that obedience to God means obedience to the laws of the state. When the devil was given free reign, people were always talking about being obsessed or possessed. Nowadays the devil does not emerge from his abode. Then miracles and prophecies were necessary. Now they are discredited. A man who publicly foretold calamities would be placed in a madhouse. The founders secretly collected money from the faithful, but now a man who collected money for his own purposes without the authorization of the law would answer for his actions before a court of justice. Thus, we no longer use any of the scaffoldings that were used in building the edifice.

Fifth question: apart from our own holy religion, which is doubtlessly the only good one, which would be the least objectionable? Would it not be the one that would stress morality and minimize dogmas; that would tend to make men just without making them absurd; that would not prescribe a belief in things impossible, contradictory, injurious to the divinity, and pernicious to mankind; that would not dare threaten with eternal torment whoever possesses common sense? Would it not be the one that would not use executioners to uphold its beliefs and that would not inundate the earth with blood on account of unintelligible sophisms; that would not allow an ambiguous expression, a play on words, and two or three fictitious charters to make a sovereign and a god of an incestuous priest, a murderer and a poisoner; that would not subject kings to this priest; that would teach simply the worship of one god, justice, tolerance, and humanity?

RESURRECTION

We are told that the Egyptians built their pyramids only for use as tombs, and that their embalmed bodies waited there for their souls to come and reanimate them after a thousand years. But if their bodies were supposed to be re-animated, why did the embalmers begin their work by piercing the skull with a hook and drawing out the brain? The notion of coming to life again without brains suggests that the Egyptians had very few while alive. . . .

The belief in resurrection goes far beyond historical times. Athalides, the son of Mercury, could die and come to life again at will; Aesculapius revived Hippolytus, and Hercules, Alcestis. Pelops, cut in pieces by his father, was resuscitated by the gods. Plato relates that Ceres came to life again for only two weeks. It was not until long after Plato that the Pharisees adopted the dogma of the Resurrection. . . . St. Augustine believed that children, and even stillborn infants, would be resuscitated full grown. Origen, Jerome, Athanasius, Basil, and others did not believe that women would be resuscitated with their sex organs. In short, there has always been disagreement concerning what we have been, what we are, and what we shall be.

RIGHT AND WRONG

Who gave us the sentiment of right and wrong? God, who gave us a brain and a heart. But how does our reason inform us that something is a vice or a virtue? Just as it informs us that two and two are four. There is no such thing as innate knowledge, just as there is no tree that springs from the soil laden with leaves and fruit. Nothing is innate or fully developed at the outset; but—this point bears repetition—God causes us to be born with organs which, as they develop, make us sense everything necessary for the conservation of the species. . . .

Jesus taught no metaphysical dogmas, He wrote no theological treatises. He did not say, "I am consubstantial; I have two wills and two natures with only one person." To the Cordeliers and the Jacobins, who were to appear twelve hundred years after him, He left the delicate and difficult task of deciding whether His mother was conceived in original sin. He never said a word about concomitant grace. He suggested neither monks nor inquisitors. He ordained nothing of what we see today.

God had made known right and wrong throughout all the ages that preceded Christianity. God has never changed and cannot change. Our inner being, our principles of reason and morality will ever be the same. How is virtue enhanced by theological distinctions, by dogmas grounded on these distinctions, or by persecutions grounded on these dogmas? Nature, alarmed and terrified by all these barbarous inventions, cries out to all men, "Be righteous men, not persecuting sophists."

S

SECT

Every sect, no matter what form it takes, is a rallying point for doubt and error. Scotist, Thomist, Realist, Nominalist, Papist, Calvinist, Molinist, and Jansenist are simply battle cries.

There is no sect in geometry; we never say a Euclidian, an Archimedian. When truth is evident, people cannot be divided into parties and factions. . . .

What would the true religion be if Christianity did not exist? That in which there are no sects; that in which all minds are necessarily in agreement. Now in what doctrine are all minds agreed? In the worship of one god and in probity. Every philosopher in the world who has ever professed a religion has said there is one god who must be just. This, then, is the universal religion established for all times and for all men. The religion on which they all agree is then true, and the systems that set them apart from each other are, therefore, false.

SELF-LOVE

A beggar in the suburbs of Madrid boldly asked for alms. A passerby said to him, "Aren't you ashamed to carry on this unworthy trade when you are able to work?" "Sir," answered the beggar, "I'm asking you for money, not for advice." With that he turned his back to the passerby, his Castilian dignity unruffled. This beggar was a haughty gentleman whose vanity was wounded by the slightest offense. He sought alms for love of himself and would not tolerate a reprimand on account of another kind of self-love. A missionary who was traveling in India met a fakir lying on his stomach, as naked as a monkey except for his chains. He was lashing himself for the sins of his Indian compatriots, who were giving him some coins. "What self-renunciation!" said one of the spectators. "Self-renunciation!" said the fakir. "I'm lashing myself in this world so that I can lash you in the next, when you will be the horses and I the rider."

Those who have said that self-love is the basis of all our sentiments and actions—whether in India, in Spain, or in any part of the habitable world—were right. And since no one has ever bothered to write in order to prove to men that they have faces, there is no need to prove to them that they have self-love. This self-love is the instrument of our preservation. It also resembles the instrument for the perpetuation of our species; it is necessary, it is dear to us, it gives us pleasure, and it must be concealed.

SENSATION

It may be that the inhabitants of other globes possess sensations unknown to us. It is possible that the number of senses increases from globe to globe, and that the being with innumerable and perfect senses is the ultimate being. . . .

Thinking amazes us, but sensation is no less miraculous. A divine power is at work in the sensation of the meanest insect as well as in the brain of a Newton. Still, if a thousand animals die before our eyes, we are not disturbed by what happens to their faculty of sensation, though it is the work of the Supreme Being. We look upon them as machines of nature created to perish and to be replaced by other machines....

All the ancients maintained that our understanding contained only what had been received by our senses. Against this, Descartes asserted in his fairy tales that we had metaphysical ideas before we found our nurse's breast. A faculty of theology proscribed this doctrine, not because it was erroneous, but because it was new. The faculty later adopted the erroneous doctrine because it had been discredited by Locke, the English philosopher, and because they assumed that Englishmen were always in the wrong. Finally, after switching opinions often, it again proscribed this ancient truth that the senses were the gateways to understanding. The faculty has acted like deeply indebted governments which sometimes honor and sometimes dishonor their notes. But the notes of this faculty have not been honored for a long time.

SOCRATIC LOVE

Early in life members of one sex are attracted to members of the other sex; in spite of what has been said about the women of Africa and southern Asia, however, the attraction is generally much stronger in men than in women. This is a law which nature has established for all animals. . . . Often a young boy for two or three years will resemble a beautiful girl. If he is loved, it is because nature is in error. His lover is paying a tribute to sex by attaching himself to whatever exhibits its beauty. Once age has caused the resemblance to disappear there is no longer room for error. . . .

All our knowledge of antiquity points to the conclusion that Socratic love was not an infamous passion. The word love is responsible for much misunderstanding. Those called the lovers of a young man were no different from those whom we call the minions of our princes. They were honorable youths concerned with the education of a child of distinction. Their common participation in a program of studies and military training was a healthy, ennobling practice which had been perverted into nocturnal merrymaking and sexual orgies. . . .

Sextus Empiricus and others have said that Socratic love was recommended by the laws of Persia, but they cannot cite the text of such laws nor can they find proof in the code of the Persians. Even if they could, I would still not believe it but would say that it cannot be true because it is impossible. No, it is not human nature to make a law that would contradict and outrage nature itself—a law which, if literally observed, would annihilate mankind.

SOLOMON

The name of Solomon has always been revered in the East. The works attributed to him, the annals of the Jews, and the fables of the Arabs, have carried his fame as far as the Indies. . . . The books attributed to Solomon have outlasted his temple. This is perhaps one of the greatest proofs of the strength of prejudices and of the weakness of the human mind. The name of the author was in itself sufficient to make the books respectable. They were acclaimed because they were written by a king and because this king was supposed to be the wisest of men.

The first work attributed to him is the Book of Proverbs. It is a collection of trivial, base, incoherent maxims, without taste, without selection, and without design. It is hard to believe that an enlightened king would have compiled a book of maxims in which there is no mention of the art of government, politics, or courtly manners and morals. We find, in contrast, whole chapters devoted exclusively to prostitutes who invite passersby from the streets to sleep with them. . . .

The Book of Ecclesiastes, which is attributed to Solomon, is different and is in better taste. The author of this work seems to be undeceived by visions of grandeur, tired of pleasures, and disgusted with knowledge. He is an Epicurean who repeats on every page that the just and the wicked are subject to the same accidents; that man is but a beast; that it is better not to be born than to exist; that there is no future life; and that nothing is better and more reasonable than for a man peacefully to enjoy the fruit of his labors with the woman whom he loves.

The whole book is the work of a sensual and disgusted materialist who apparently injected in the last verse an edifying word about God to lessen the scandal that such a book would necessarily create.

SOUL

It would be nice to see one's soul. "Know thyself" is an excellent precept; but only God can put it into practice. Who else can know his own essence. . . . ? The first philosophers, whether Chaldeans or Egyptians, put it this way: We must have within ourselves something which produces our thoughts; this something must be very subtle—a breath, a fire, an ether, a quintessence, a slender simulacrum, an entelechy, a number, a harmony. Finally, according to the divine Plato, it consists of *like* and *unlike* qualities. Epicurus, quoting Democritus, said, "We have within us thinking." But how, my friend, does an atom think? The truth is that you do not know. . . . It is highly significant that in the laws of God's chosen people not one word is said about the spirituality and immortality of the soul. . . . If Moses had announced the dogma of the immortality of the soul, a great number of Jews would not have unremittingly combatted it. The great school of the Sadducees would not have been authorized in the state. The Sadducees would not have filled the highest offices, nor would great pontiffs have been selected from their ranks. . . .

"Oh, mortal! God has endowed you with understanding to enable you to conduct yourself prudently, not to delve into the essence of the things that He has created." That was the belief of Locke, and before Locke Gazanda, and before Gazanda a host of sages. But we now have bachelors who know all the things which were unknown to those great men.

SOVEREIGN GOOD

The sovereign good is that which brings us such intense delight as to render us incapable of feeling anything else, just as the greatest evil is that which goes so far as to rob us of all feeling. Those are the two extremes of human nature, and neither of them can long endure. Neither extreme delight nor extreme suffering can last a lifetime. The sovereign good, like the sovereign evil, is nothing more than a chimera.

STATES—GOVERNMENTS

Which is the best form of government? Everyone I have ever known has governed some state. I am not speaking of ministers of state who actually govern, some for two or three years, others for six months, and others for six weeks; I am speaking rather of all the other men who, in the dining room or in the drawing room, unfold their systems of government, reorganizing armies, the church, the judiciary, and finances. . . .

In France, Spain, and England learned men, worthy perhaps of governing, have written about the administration of states. Their books have done much good. To be sure, they have not reformed the ministers serving at the time of their publication, for a minister does not and cannot reform himself; he is a grown man with no need of further instructions or advice; he has no time to listen to others; he must devote full time to the affairs of state. But these good books mold young people destined to hold high offices. They mold the princes and statesmen of the succeeding generation.

The strong and weak points of every type of government have recently been studied. Tell me, then, you who have traveled and read and observed, in which state or under which type of government would you prefer to be born? I suppose that a landed lord in France would not be displeased if born in Germany, for he would be a sovereign instead of a subject. A peer of France would enjoy the privileges of the English peerage: he would be a legislator. The jurist and the financier would fare better in France then elsewhere. But what would be the choice of a learned man—a free, unbiased man with a modest fortune?

"But once more," said the European, "which state would you choose?" The Brahmin answered, "The state in which only the laws are obeyed." "That is an old answer," said the counselor. "But still a good one," said the Brahmin. "And where is that country?" said the counselor. The Brahmin answered, "We must search for it."

SUPERSTITION

Almost everything that goes beyond the worship of the Supreme Being and submission of the heart to His eternal decrees is superstition. . . . One superstition which may be pardonable and may even encourage virtue is that of deifying great men who have been benefactors to mankind. It would doubtlessly be better to restrict ourselves to looking upon great men as venerable men, and above all to emulate them. We ought to venerate but not to worship a Solon, a Thales, or a Pythagoras. We certainly ought not to worship a Hercules for having cleaned out the Augean stables and for having bedded down with fifty women in one night. . . .

The superstitious man is to the knave what the slave is to the tyrant. Moreover, he is governed by the fanatic and becomes a fanatic. The superstition that was born of paganism and adopted by Judaism infected the Christian church at the beginning. All the Fathers of the Church without exception believed in the power of magic. The Church always condemned magic but always believed in it; the Church excommunicated sorcerers, not as aberrant madmen, but as men actually in league with devils.

Today, one-half of Europe believes that the other half has long been and still is superstitious. The Protestants look upon the relics, indulgences, macerations, prayers for the dead, holy water, and almost all the rites of the Roman Church as superstitious folly. Superstition, according to them, consists of mistaking useless practices for necessary ones. . . .

Can people ever be freed of all their superstitious prejudices? This is another way of asking whether there can ever be a nation of philosophers.

T

THEIST

The Theist is a man firmly persuaded of the existence of a Supreme Being who is good and powerful, and who has shaped all things, vegetating, sentient, and reflecting; who perpetuates their species, punishes their crimes without cruelty, and rewards virtuous deeds with kindness.

The Theist does not know how God punishes or rewards or pardons, for he is not rash enough to feel that he understands how God acts; but he knows that God does act and that he is just. The arguments against Providence do not shake his faith, for they are only arguments, not proofs. He believes in Providence although he is aware of it only through its effects and appearances; and judging the things that he does not see by the things that he sees, he thinks that Providence extends throughout all places and all ages.

United in this principle with the rest of the universe, he joins none of the sects, for they are all mutually exclusive. His religion is the most ancient and the most far-reaching; for simple adoration of one God preceded all the systems in the world. He speaks a language all nations understand, even though they are unable to understand each other. His brothers are found from Peiping to Cayenne, and among them are numbered all the sages.

THEOLOGIAN

I once knew a true theologian. He had mastered the languages of the East and knew as much as could be known about the ancient rites of different nations. . . . He distinguished between policy and wisdom, between pride that seeks to subjugate minds and the desire for self-illumination, between zeal and fanaticism. . . . He finally achieved knowledge unknown to the greater part of his colleagues. The more learned he became, however, the more he mistrusted all that he knew. While he lived he was indulgent; and at death, he confessed that his life had been spent in vain.

TOLERANCE

What is tolerance? It is the appanage of mankind. We are all riddled by shortcomings and error. Let us forgive each other's follies; that is the first law of nature. . . .

Of all religions, the Christian ought doubtlessly to inspire the most tolerance, although Christians have always been the most intolerant of men. . . . Theudas and Judas were called Messiahs before Jesus; and Dositheus, Simon, and Menander called themselves Messiahs after Jesus. During the first century in the history of the Church, and even before the name of Christian was known, there were a score of sects in Judea.

The contemplative Gnostics, the Dositheans, the Cerinthians existed before Jesus' disciples had taken the name of Christians. There were some thirty gospels, each belonging to a different society; and by the end of the first century, thirty sects of Christians had sprung up in Asia Minor, in Syria, in Alexandria, and even in Rome. . . . Dissension is the greatest evil that afflicts mankind, and tolerance is its sole remedy. . . . If there is one sect that reminds us of the time of the first Christians, it is undeniably the Quaker. . . . But in all its ceremonies and doctrines the Catholic, Apostolic, and Roman religion is the reverse of the religion of Jesus.

TORTURE

Though there are few articles on jurisprudence in these unpretentious alphabetical reflections, we must say a few words about torture, otherwise known as interrogation. This is a strange manner of questioning men. Its inventors were not, however, simple curiosity seekers. There is every indication that this part of our legal system owes its origin to highwaymen. . . . Conquerors who succeeded these highwaymen found their invention useful in advancing their own interests and resorted to it whenever they suspected that someone had an evil intention—for example, that of being free. . . . The French, who are reputed, I know not why, to be a very humane people, are amazed that the English, who had the inhumanity to take from us all of Canada, have renounced the pleasure of using torture. . . .

The Russians were looked upon as barbarians in 1700. This is only the year 1769, and yet their empress has just given to this great state laws which would do honor to Minos, Numa, or Solon if they had been intelligent enough to invent them. The most noteworthy is universal tolerance; second comes the abolition of torture. Justice and humanity have guided her pen, she has reformed everything. Woe to a nation which, though long civilized, is still governed by outmoded, atrocious customs! "Why should we change our legal system?" we ask. "Europe accepts our cooks, our tailors, and our wig makers. This proves that our laws are good."

TRANSUBSTANTIATION

Protestants, and especially philosophical Protestants, regard transubstantiation as the epitome of impudence in monks and of imbecility in laymen. They will accept no part of this belief, which they call monstrous, and they maintain that it is impossible for a sensible man who has given thought to the matter to accept it in good faith. "It is," they say, "so absurd, so contrary to every physical law, and so contradictory that God Himself could not carry out this operation, since to assume that He is capable of inconsistency is in effect to annihilate Him. . . ." Their horror increases when they are told that monks in Catholic countries rise from their incestuous beds and with their hands still defiled by uncleanliness make gods by the hundreds, eat and drink them, and digest and excrete them. But when they realize that this superstition, a thousand times more absurd and sacrilegious than those of the Egyptians, produces for an Italian priest some fifteen to twenty millions of revenue, they are ready to take up arms and march against the priest in the palace of the Caesars.

TYRANNY

Tyrant is the name given to a sovereign who knows no law other than his own whims, who takes the property of his subjects, and who afterwards conscripts them to go and take that of their neighbors. There are no such tyrants in Europe. There is a difference between individual tyranny and collective tyranny. Collective tyranny exists when one body invades the rights of other bodies and exercises despotism through the laws which it corrupts. Nor are there tyrants of this kind in Europe.

Under which tyranny would you prefer to live? Under neither. But if it were necessary to choose, I would detest individual tyranny less than collective tyranny. A despot always has some good moments; a group of despots, never. If one wrongs me, I can disarm him through his mistress, his confessor, or his pages; but a company of brave tyrants cannot be disarmed through any such stratagem. . . . How must I act? I fear that in this world we run the risk of having to choose between being either the anvil or the hammer. Happy is he who can escape this choice!

V

VIRTUE

What is virtue? Beneficence toward your neighbor. Can anything other than that which is good for me be called virtue? I am independent, you are generous; I am in danger, you come to my rescue; I am wrong, and you correct me; I feel neglected, and you console me; I am ignorant, and you teach me. In all these instances I would have no hesitancy in calling you virtuous. But what of the cardinal and theological virtues. . . ? Your theological virtues are heavenly gifts; your cardinal virtues are excellent qualities that serve as guides, but they are not virtues in relation to your neighbor. A prudent man does good for himself; a virtuous man does good for other men. St. Paul was right in saying that charity is superior to both faith and hope.

W

WAR

Famine, pestilence, and war are the three most famous
ingredients in this nether world. . . . The most determined
flatterer will easily agree that war always entails pestilence
and famine. . . . The wonderful thing about this infernal
enterprise is that the leader of each group of murderers has
his banners blessed and solemnly invokes God before going
out to exterminate his neighbor. . . . Natural religion has
prevented citizens a thousand times from committing crimes.
A civilized person lacks the will; a sensitive person becomes
alarmed at the notion of a just and avenging God; but an
artificial religion encourages all cruelties practiced by troops—
conspiracies, sedition, pillaging, ambuscades, the sacking of
towns, robberies, and murder. Each advances gaily to crime
under the banner of his saint. . . .

WICKED

Humanity, beneficence, modesty, temperance, kindness,
wisdom, pity—what becomes of these and what do they mean

to me if half a pound of lead shot from a distance of six hundred paces mutilates my body and I die at the age of twenty, suffering unspeakable torments in the midst of five or six thousand dying men? Or if, on opening my eyes for the last time, I see the town in which I was born destroyed by fire and sword, and the last sounds to reach my ears are the cries of women and children expiring beneath the ruins, all for the pretended interests of an unknown man?

We are told that human nature is essentially perverse, that man is a child of the devil, and wicked. Nothing is more unsound; for, my friend, you who preach to me that everyone is born perverse warn me by the same breath that you, too, are born perverse and that I must mistrust you as I would a fox or a crocodile. "Oh, no," you say. "I am regenerated. I am neither a heretic nor an infidel. You can trust me." But you think that the rest of the human race, which you call heretics or infidels consists of groups of monsters; and that whenever you speak to Lutherans or Turks you can be sure that they will rob and murder you, since they are children of the devil. They were born wicked; one has not been regenerated and the other has degenerated. But it would be more logical and much more fitting to say to men, "You were born good; see how dreadful it would be to corrupt the purity of your being. . . ."

Man is not born wicked; he becomes wicked just as he becomes sick. . . . Bring together all the children of the universe and you will see in them only annoyance, mildness, and fear; if they were born wicked, mischievous, and cruel, they would give some indication of it, just as little serpents try to bite. . . . It follows that man is not born bad. Why, then, are many men afflicted by the scourge of wickedness? The reason is that those who are at their head are afflicted by the malady and communicate it to them, just as a woman afflicted with the disease that Christopher Columbus brought back from America spreads this venom throughout Europe. The first ambitious man corrupted the earth.

INDEX